Imagining AMERICA

Imagining AMERICA

Paul Thai's Journey From The Killing Fields Of Cambodia To Freedom In The U.S.A.

SHARON SLOAN FIFFER

Paragon House

NEW YORK

First edition, 1991
Published in the United States by
Paragon House
90 Fifth Avenue
New York, NY 10011
Copyright © 1991 by Sharon Sloan Fiffer

Manufactured in the United States of America
10 9 8 7 6 5 4 3 2 1

Library of Congress Cataloging-in-Publication Data

Fiffer, Sharon Sloan
     Imagining America : Paul Thai's journey from
the killing fields of Cambodia to freedom in the
U.S.A. / Sharon Sloan Fiffer. —1st ed.
     p.   cm.
     Includes bibliographical references.
     ISBN 1-55778-326-8 : $19.95
     1. Thai, Paul.   2. Cambodian American—Tex-
as—Dallas—Biography.   3. Refugees, Political—
Texas—Dallas—Biography.   4. Police—Texas—
Dallas—Biography.   5.   Dallas
(Tex.)—Biography.   I. Title.
F394.D219K45   1991   91–2030
                                          CIP

For my husband, Steve Fiffer, whose insight, support, and love—freely given and wisely timed—made this book come true.

And for all Cambodians, living here and living there. I hope that telling Paul's story will help Americans understand you better and that it will enable you to write better endings to your own life stories.

ជូនចំពោះប្រជាពលរដ្ឋខ្មែរទាំងអស់ ដែលរស់នៅក្នុងសហរដ្ឋអាមេរិក ស្រុកខ្មែរ និងទីលំនៅនានា។

ខ្ញុំសង្ឃឹមថា ការរៀបរាប់អំពីរឿងរបស់លោក ផល់ ថៃ (ៗ) អាចជួយជនជាតិអាមេរិក ឲ្យយល់អំពីទុក្ខវេទនារបស់លោកអ្នក និងជើម្បីអាចជួយឲ្យអ្នកទាំងអស់គ្នា ឲ្យមានសុភមង្គលល្អក្នុងនាគជីវិត។

Contents

Acknowledgments   ix

Introduction   xi

Imagination   xv

Chapter 1   America Was Our Dream   1

Chapter 2   Year Zero   11

Chapter 3   He Called Me Mr. Thai   36

Chapter 4   Two Escapes   61

Chapter 5   Cops   88

Chapter 6   And Robbers   109

Chapter 7   A New American   123

Chapter 8   Police Academy II   149

Chapter 9   Deep Night   161

Chapter 10   Reinventing the Dream   173

Epilogue   And That Is Freedom   185

Reality 1991   197

For Further Reading   199

Acknowledgments

Paul Thai and his wife, Marina, opened their hearts and their home to me. Since this book is Paul's story, it is obvious that it could not have been written without his cooperation. Less obvious is the fact that he gave up an enormous amount of time and energy to devote himself to the project. Marina, Chet, and Maly also gave of themselves so that this story could be told. I thank the family for their openness, their honesty, and their friendship.

I would also like to thank the following people who graciously contributed their thoughts and feelings to this book: Ron and Melinda Cowart, Charles Kemp, Charles Morris, Leck Keovilay, Thao Dam, Kevin Lim, John Lim, Ernestine Gaitan, Syl Bennison, Lance Raisbridge, Barbara Boyd, the members of the Dallas Police Department, in particular, Deputy Chief Rudy Diaz, who put me in touch with Sergeant Dan Bell at the storefront, Lynn Dorsey, and Clarence McClenton.

Thanks to Rebecca Yane and Kompha Seth from the Cambodian Association of Chicago.

Thanks to my friends, Thom Bishop and Lois Hauselman, who read the manuscript in various stages and gave me advice, encouragement, and support.

Chris Messenger read the entire manuscript with incredible care and gave me valuable and extensive criticism. My thanks are a small token for his friendship and his insight.

Catherine Rooney took excellent photographs and has been my friend for over twenty-five years. Thanks for both.

Thanks to my agent, Carol Mann; my editor, PJ Dempsey; and editor in chief, Ken Stuart of Paragon House.

Thanks to Pam Parker for her enthusiasm and excellent transcribing skills.

Thanks to my late friend, Dolores Weinberg, editor of the literary magazine, *Other Voices*, who grudgingly and lovingly gave me time off to write the book and to Lois Hauselman and Fran Podulka who did my work. Thanks to Dr. Lesley Kordecki at Barat College for generously allowing me flexibility in my teaching schedule to accommodate my writing timetable.

For helping me keep my family and household together during the writing of the book, I thank all my friends and family, especially Rose Rainer, Elaine Fiffer, and Judy Groothuis.

My husband, Steve, not only brought the project home to me, but also encouraged me, counseled me and believed in me. I thank Kate Fiffer, Nora Fiffer, and Robert Fiffer for their cooperation and understanding.

And a special thanks to my father, Donald Schmidt. Oddly enough my American-born father believed the same thing as Paul's father—that America meant freedom and education. He told me once that his only religion was a belief in education and educating his children. He also advised me to read more than one newspaper a day. Like Paul's father, he taught me not to be a frog in a well.

Introduction

In 1492, Columbus sailed the ocean blue . . .

In 1992, Americans will celebrate the five hundredth anniversary of the discovery of their country by Christopher Columbus. Already, T-shirts are being lettered, coffee mugs are being emblazoned. Although there will be several serious books, documentaries, and more than a few elementary and secondary school social studies projects centered on Columbus, the discovery of America, and the controversy that surrounds the issue, most Americans will be reminded of their history in the usual manner—through popular culture. Television, radio, music, movies, videos, cartoons, advertising, and merchandising will remind consumers that this is America's big birthday and that now is the time—the one and only time—to stock up on Columbus's Discovery collectibles.

Discovering America, however, was not and is not a onetime event. Discovering America is a process that is continually explored in the work of historians, social scientists, anthropologists, philosophers, and poets. And on another level, discovering America is the job of television programmers, commercial filmmakers, and market researchers.

Discovering America is also the dream and the task of the refugee.

Paul Thai was born in Cambodia. He survived the tortures and abuses of Pol Pot's Khmer Rouge regime—the labor camps and the killing fields—then escaped into the new horrors of the refugee camps along the Thai–Cambodian border. In 1981, with his parents, seven of his brothers, and his sister, Paul Thai, 18 years old, came to his dream land—America. Unlike Columbus who explored by choice and would sail home to Europe, Paul had to continue to discover America, to make it his home. His experiences help define America for the American-born citizens as well as the new Americans who arrive here daily; the immigrants, eager to better their lives and expand their opportunities, and the refugees, confused, hurt, broken, and home*land*less.

Paul Thai's story of survival, struggle, and success would be valuable at any time, but is essential today. In the 1980s, the U.S. Asian population increased by seventy percent. Asian-Americans numbered about 6.5 million on July 1, 1988, up from 3.8 million eight years earlier. New Americans from Cambodia, Laos, Vietnam, China, Taiwan, Hong Kong, the Phillipines, South Korea, and Micronesia are now our neighbors in America. In order to get to know us better, the new Americans become close observers of the America that is accessible to them—the television families who come into their living rooms daily in soap operas and nightly in situation comedies. And in turn, American-born Americans often accept the sterotyped Asian whiz kids, the miracle minority, as the typical Asian–American. Getting to know Paul Thai as an individual and seeing America through his family's eyes should be an obligation. Paul's story encourages us to extend a hand, person-to-person, which, in turn, offers us the chance to be true neighbors. Equally important, it encourages an open friendship which might be the only way to dispel the myths surrounding the "typical American family" as produced by American television.

When my husband, writer Steve Fiffer, returned from a research trip to Dallas, he spent hours telling me about an unusual police station—the East Dallas Storefront—and his meeting with Corporal Ron Cowart and Paul Thai, Leck Keovilay, and Thao Dam. He described the daily interworkings of the storefront and its staff, its volunteers, and its clients as a kind of American opera—voices of joy and pain mingling, soloing, soaring.

At that time, Steve had in mind a film about Ron Cowart, a Vietnam Vet, a Dallas Cop, who decides to start a storefront police station to help Asian refugees. As he and I discussed it more, the film idea spun off a book, the book turned into another book and as we read tape transcript after tape transcript, the book evolved into Paul's story . . . a story that I would write.

After some years of teaching American literature, I couldn't help but hear that American opera, too. I kept thinking of Walt Whitman who celebrated America and told us all about America singing its varied carols. I listened to Paul's voice, wracked with the pain of his past and at the same time, filled with his joy at being an American. I began to wonder what that American opera sounded like to him.

I began listening harder to the voices around me . . . those of my family, my students, my friends, my colleagues, my senators, my congressmen, my president. I listened to the voices of the television, the movies and the radio. And the idea of an American opera that Steve and I had discussed so easily became a complicated, deafening roar of conflicting sounds. And that seemed as good a place to start as any—America as a deafening roar of conflicting sounds—what did it sound like to Paul Thai?

Luckily for me, Paul is an excellent listener. He has been and continues to be a keen observer of Americans—their habits, their words, their actions. In writing Paul's story and attempting to translate some of his experiences into a kind of side trip into the American culture, I hope that a deeper picture of America emerges. I am not the first writer to speculate that America is best defined by its immigrants, but I would like to be the last who has to suggest that the American conscience should be shaped by its refugees.

Daily, during interviews at the East Dallas storefront and at Paul's apartment in Little Asia, as I sat listening to taped conversations and when I actually began writing the book, I labored over the question—how does someone become an American? What is an American? Who is an American? Learning American English, as it stands and as it evolves, is only the beginning of a lifetime process that by its very nature ends up defining the American culture. For better or worse. There are few Americans who want to be defined as the characters portrayed by the actors of "General Hospital," "Who's the Boss?" or "Dallas," yet for those with limited English, who rarely glimpse the inside of a real American household, television programs often provide the American model. If that seems as if it would be confusing for immigrants and refugees, imagine the double confusion for those in a cable viewing area. Several cable channels rerun older shows from the so-called "golden age" of television comedy. Although it may be amusing and nostalgic for some American-born Americans to watch Donna Reed run her household or Dobie Gillis chase girls, it hardly gives an accurate portrait of life in the 1990s— particularly the life of Southeast Asian refugees in Dallas, Texas.

When I was given the opportunity to write *Imagining America*, I knew all the things I did not want it to be. It would not be an academic treatise on the state of American culture or an exploration of the U.S. Government's Southeast Asian policy. Nor would it be a sociological text examining the stages of the assimilation of the American immigrant. It would not be a traditional biography—if a traditional biographical form truly exists. Neither would it be the exaltation of a famous figure, or a celebrity exposé. It would simply be, I hoped, Paul Thai's life examined—examined both within the cultural context of Cambodia and the United States. It would allow the reader to discover Paul Thai as Paul Thai discovers America.

Paul Thai's life, like that of every Cambodian alive today, has been filled with pain. He has witnessed unspeakable acts and suffered unimaginable torture. But the story of his life up to the present and into the future is curiously upbeat. It is his strength, his humor, his intelligence and his own curiosity that keep him moving forward, not rooted in his devastating Cambodian past, but growing into his promising Cambodian-American future. Paul's story is compelling not only because of the events that shaped it, but because of his own independent grace, his ability to now shape his own destiny.

On July 18, 1990, the federal government announced that the United States would officially change its policy toward Cambodia and Vietnam. Since the current Cambodian administration had been put into place by the Vietnamese "liberators" who defeated the Khmer Rouge in 1979, the United States, because it had not recognized Vietnam, had not recognized the Vietnamese-backed Hun Sen government of Cambodia. Instead, it had allied itself with the Cambodian guerrilla coalition, which includes the Communist Khmer Rouge. Secretary of State James Baker stated that a change was necessary because existing American policy appeared increasingly likely to promote a return to power of the Khmer Rouge, under whose rule in the 1970s more than a million Cambodians were killed or died of starvation.

I, like so many others who are horrified that a second holocaust could occur in this century, hope that it is not too late.

—Sharon Sloan Fiffer

Imagination

It is too easy to imagine waking up on the moon where nothing looks the same or in a land where no one speaks your language.

Imagine this instead.

Imagine you've never heard of the Beatles. Or Mozart. Or Michael Jordan, William F. Buckley, Oprah Winfrey, Little Orphan Annie, or Mickey Mouse. You've never heard of Elvis or Babe Ruth or Shirley Temple or Groucho Marx or Johnny Carson.

Imagine you don't celebrate birthdays, nor do you celebrate Christmas, Chanukha, or New Year's on December 31. You've never stuffed a turkey. You do not Trick or Treat.

Imagine you've never seen "I Love Lucy," *Gone with the Wind,* "Ozzie and Harriet," "Gilligan's Island," Bill Cosby, "The Simpsons," "Cheers," "L.A. Law," or any Saturday morning cartoons.

Imagine you've never read *The New York Times, The National Enquirer, Newsweek,* or *Mad.*

Imagine you've never seen designer labels, television commercials, advertising billboards. You've never heard of "trickle-down," "supply side," "small print," or "bottom lines."

Imagine you've never heard of cholesterol or calories or stair-climbing machines or spa cuisine. You've never heard of brunch.

Imagine starting over in a land where language depends on a shared consciousness not only of nature, spirituality, art, manners, and humanity, but on a shared knowledge of and nostalgia for television, sports, music, and film.

Imagine, after having your own homeland destroyed before your eyes, building a new life in a land where you have to learn a new language—one that is so self-referential—that you must learn not only the words, but the memories.

Imagine you've seen your family tortured to death. Imagine watching your first music video on MTV. Imagine coming to America . . .

Imagining
AMERICA

1

America Was Our Dream

The United States themselves are essentially the greatest poem.
—Walt Whitman, Preface to the 1855 *Leaves of Grass*

Paul Thai, his father and mother, his six brothers and one sister, walked unsteadily through the jetway into Dallas/Fort Worth Airport in the middle of a humid July night, 1981. The family had just experienced their first airplane ride, a trip from Bangkok to Texas that lasted more than thirty hours. It was a journey that took them from fear, misery, and starvation to the great mysterious hope of America.

"Freedom and education. That is what America meant to us," says Paul. "An old man in the labor camp had whispered it to me a long time ago, during the Communist time. 'A-mer-i-ca,' he said. When I saw my father again, I asked him about America and he said he, too, had heard of America. He said he didn't know much about it . . . he just knew that it was the land of freedom and education."

Paul doesn't know where his father, a Cambodian restaurant owner who masqueraded as a peasant farmer to escape the Khmer Rouge purge of light-skinned, soft-handed town people, first learned about America, but to Paul, it doesn't matter. "America was our dream, and it stayed our dream." In a time of nightmares, when over one million Cambodians were murdered outright or beaten, tortured, and starved to death, Paul clearly knew the value of a pure, unadulterated dream.

After one unsuccessful, disastrous attempt to escape Cambodia in 1979, the Thai family tried again and ended up at Khao I Dang camp located on the

Thai–Cambodian border, remaining there for about nine months. In 1981 they were transferred to Mairut Camp. The Thai family, like other hopeful residents of the camp, wrote a steady stream of letters, searching for a group to sponsor them to come to America. "We wrote to everyone, every organization we heard about. Then we got a letter from the International Rescue Committee (IRC) saying they would be our sponsor," remembers Paul.

At Mairut Camp, there was a big bulletin board where someone, twice a day, posted the names and destinations of those families who were scheduled to depart. Paul sat in front of the board every day. "Nothing else to do anyway. And one day, I see my father's name, and I am so excited. Some people see that they are going to California and they are so happy. They say, 'Oh California is so nice! And warm—it has weather just like Cambodia.' And when I see we are going to Dallas, Texas, I say that and someone says to me, 'Oh no, you are going to Dallas? Don't you know that is where President Kennedy was shot?' And I think, oh no. Then someone says, 'Yeah, in Texas they got cowboys who will shoot you down in the street.' So I go and tell my father this and he says he would rather be shot by a cowboy in America than by the Khmer Rouge in Cambodia, so we stay happy about coming to America. Dallas, Texas, America."

Paul tells these stories in English spoken with the precision characteristic of a careful new speaker of a language. Not so characteristic is the Texas drawl that creeps into certain words and phrases. Paul is delighted when others notice it. "I am a Texan now," he nods.

That first night, at the airport, Paul's father held up a sign with their family name written on it, so that the International Rescue Committee caseworker would recognize them and take them to their new home in America. No one in their family spoke a word of English. No one on the plane spoke a word of Khmer, the language of Cambodia. "Everyone was so nice to us, though," Paul remembers. "The flight attendants kept asking us questions and smiling. We couldn't understand anything, but we were so happy and excited. Confused, too, because we left early in the morning on the plane, then it got dark for only a few hours, then it was light again, and we didn't understand."

Although they knew that some families were flown to the Phillipines for a six-month course of study in both language and United States culture, Paul's family flew directly to Dallas. They were never told why they would not have some instruction before their arrival in America, but they were too anxious to get to their new land to be concerned.

"We had three days after we saw our name on the board. That was after we had already moved from Mairut Camp, to Transit Center, then to Lumpani. They told us to pack and be ready then. But we have nothing, so we are ready to come right away. We sat and waited with our box—my mother had some pans, some dishes, I think, and I think maybe we had a few books. My father had saved some clothes from the Communist time, they were just rags, just black rags and we said, no, we don't want that, but my father said yes, we save them for the memory. So that was it. We were ready. We asked, 'Why three days to prepare to leave? We don't even need three hours.' "

While the family waited for the sponsor to find them, Paul says they looked at the Americans. "Thousands of Americans here at the airport, it seemed like to us. And we loved it! And all the lights! We looked out at the lights of the city and it was like heaven with all those lights. We really felt like we were born again. But some people, you know, were confused, felt lost, felt airsick from the plane. There were those who had never seen glass before. Like all those big windows and glass doors at the airport. People walked right into glass and bumped their heads. Some people looked at the escalator and just shook their heads. They took the stairs instead!"

The IRC caseworker drove Paul and his family to a house where they would spend their first night. The lights of the tall city buildings that had seemed so heaven-like remained visible, but distant. The neighborhood where Paul's family would be living was one mile east of downtown Dallas.

After the Refugee Act of 1980 (a statute declaring that the United States openly welcomes political refugees internationally) was implemented, Asian enclaves grew seemingly overnight in large cities and wherever else sponsors such as IRC could be found. Dallas's "Little Asia" became the home of approximately four thousand Southeast Asian immigrants. Cambodians, Laotians, and Vietnamese were crowded into dilapidated, substandard housing in the one-square-mile area.

Paul's family spent their first night in America sharing a small two-bedroom house with two other Cambodian families. The caseworker who brought them there from the airport flicked the electric lights off and on, showed them the stove, turning the gas on and off, and opened the cupboards and refrigerator to show them the rice and chickens that were there for them to cook if they were hungry. After demonstrating the water taps—one hot, one cold—and how the toilet flushed, he had to leave, promising to return in the morning to help them find an apartment of their own.

"We were too excited to sleep that night. We stayed up and talked. Talked about being in America and how we were so happy. My mother cried, though. She was happy, but we still have a brother in Cambodia, and she cried because we were here and he was there."

Two days later, the caseworker returned with good news. An apartment had been reserved for the Thai family and they were going to move there right away. Other families needed to use the space at the "welcome house," so they were asked to pack up immediately.

Their new home wasn't far from the interim housing used by the IRC. The apartment at 5027 Live Oak Avenue looked wonderful to the family. The lack of a yard, the paper thin walls went unnoticed. The missing locks on the mailboxes in the hall, the peeling paint, the worn out appliances were unimportant. They celebrated having rooms of their own. "Two bedrooms!" Paul remembers excitedly. Two bedrooms for their family of ten.

"It was hot in there. July and no air conditioner that worked. But we didn't feel like we could complain. We were in America, in our own apartment, so we were happy. That night, though, none of us could sleep because we were so hot. We children all slept in the living room, on mats on the floor. My mother got a pan of cool water and she stayed up all night, going from one of us to the other, sponging us off, cooling us down so we could rest. She stayed up and did that every night in the summer heat." Paul nods as he says this about his mother, adding a soft "yup" afterward, considering the memory. "My six brothers and my sister, all of us, she made sure we could sleep, so we would be ready to work and go to school."

Paul's oldest living brother, Mao, had arrived in America one month before the rest of his family. The caseworker expected that he would help his parents and brothers and sister, show them around the neighborhood, help them find the food stores, the IRC offices where they could begin the process of finding jobs. Mao was eager to show the family around Little Asia, and even more eager that they should have a true American home. Every morning of his first month alone in America, Mao went out before going to his regular job and collected aluminum cans to sell so he could afford to buy his family a present when they arrived—a small, secondhand black-and-white television. His brothers and sisters were delighted. Says Paul, "We had seen television at the home of my father's friend in Phnom Penh a long time ago, but we never saw much, saw it only maybe once a year. Never saw as much as we wanted!"

Paul says that their third night in America, in their own apartment, was just as confused and sleepless. "The heat, and the excitement! Also, our nights and days were still confused from the trip. We stayed up and talked, watched the TV. We didn't understand English, didn't know what show we were watching, but we enjoyed it anyway." The next morning, however, their viewing pleasure was abruptly cancelled. While they were gathered around the small set watching a program, a man walked into the apartment. He said nothing, but went over to the television set, unplugged it, and walked back out the door.

"We didn't know what happened really," says Paul, shaking his head. "We just sat there. It must have looked funny, all of us just sitting there looking at where the television set *was*. But we thought it must be something American that we didn't understand. Or that my brother knew about it. After about an hour, we got kind of lonely so we went to find Mao. We asked him if he sent somebody over to get the TV, and he said, 'No, I didn't send anyone,' and we told him what happened. He said, 'Oh, no,' and I said, 'What do you mean, oh, no?' and he said, 'You were robbed!' "

In *America*? Paul thought at the time that it was impossible to be robbed in America. That is what soldiers and others in Thailand did, that is what the Khmer Rouge did, marching through towns, destroying property that they didn't want to take for themselves. Those people, back there, from the past . . . those were robbers. Of childhoods, cultures, lives. But robbers in America? Unthinkable.

Paul's brother had just been to a meeting in his apartment building where a policeman had spoken, through a translator, warning the Asian immigrants that there were people who might come in and try to rob them, take advantage of them, even hurt them. That is how Mao knew that his family had been robbed. Otherwise, according to Paul, he wouldn't have known what happened either.

Mao went back to the apartment with Paul and tried to speak to the building manager. Since the building manager didn't understand Cambodian, he went to find someone who could translate. When someone came who could speak both English and Cambodian, and the crime was reported, the building manager told Paul's father he would have to call the police. Paul's father quickly said no, shepherded his family back into their apartment, and closed the door. The translator followed and spoke through the door, trying to convince the Thais that the police would attempt to get their television back for them.

"They will try to get the TV back for us? They will not try to hurt us?"

Paul remembers asking. Paul's memory of police and soldiers in Cambodia was a bad one. When an official, anyone dressed in a uniform, appeared at your family's door, something bad was going to happen. Something might be stolen or confiscated, or worse, someone, a family member, maybe your entire family, was going to disappear.

When the Dallas police officer arrived, Paul's father went out into the hall to talk to him. "He closed the door behind him and told us to lock it so that if he dies, we will live and be safe. But we peeked out anyway, and the policeman was so nice. He even shook hands with my father. We were so surprised."

The police did not recover the television set. But as Paul remembers it, "At least they were nice."

The caseworker returned to make sure that the Thais had a sofa, a working refrigerator and a table with four chairs. Paul remembers the ten family members taking turns sitting at the table. As older brother Mao was an experienced American—he had been in Dallas for one month already—much of the cultural education was left to him. But since Mao was working, much of Paul's cultural education was up to Paul.

"Our caseworker, our sponsor, gave my father about one hundred dollars to help him get us started. At least, I think it was that much. We had directions to their office and they said they would help us with schools and jobs. We also needed to apply for assistance, for food stamps. Our father gave my brother and me one dollar to go out with during the first few days. I always wanted to do the same thing. Buy apples. My brother had brought some for us the first night and we had never tasted anything so good, so sweet. So that is what I wanted to do, my brother Chi and I . . . go out and buy more apples. We could walk to do that."

Bus journeys were a more difficult adventure. "The caseworker told us the numbers of the bus we were supposed to take to the office. He says to take number 20 downtown, then get off and wait for number 9 that will take you to the office. When you go back, you take number 9 back downtown, then get on 20 to go back home. But there were many things he didn't mention, like for instance that you have to pay. It must have looked funny—bus stops, doors open, a group of Asians gets on bus, doors close, doors open, Asians get off bus. Then when we know we have to pay, we get on with dollar bills and bus driver won't take them. Must have change. We can't understand driver, driver can't understand us. Just thinks we are dumb. Then you figure out that you have to get change and get it and get back on bus, but don't know how much you are supposed to put in. So you ask driver and he doesn't understand. Pretty soon, he just wants you off the bus! So we watch. We watch people drop the coins in and we count and learn how much to drop in. Then we ride the bus. But we don't know how to get off, how to make the bus stop. So we ride and ride the bus until the driver looks at us like he thinks there's something wrong with us, so we get off. And we get on another bus and get lost. Then we walk."

Paul and the other Cambodians who emigrated to Texas were unused to the city streets, the traffic lights, the cars, the exhaust, the noise, the bustle of American city life, but they were *not* unused to walking. The Cambodians who reached American shores had walked through jungles, minefields, up mountains and down, through rivers red with blood and clotted with dead and bloated bodies, through the mass graves that once had been their countryside in order to reach the border camps where they might have a chance at getting out. A thirty-minute walk to the IRC office was quite literally a stroll in the park for these new Texans.

"When we arrived at the IRC office, sponsor would ask us why we looked so hot or so tired and we would say we walked, and they would ask why we didn't take the bus. I kept trying the bus and kept getting lost because I didn't know how to ask the bus driver to stop and let me off.

"Because I am a good Cambodian boy, I keep my head down, my eyes down, so I never see Americans pull the cord to ring the bell to signal to driver to stop. I hear the bell, and I notice that the bus stops, but by the time I look up at the sound of the bell, the cord has been pulled and I don't see how to do it. Then, one day, I am on the bus, about to be lost again, when I see an old, old lady. She is ahead of me and I see her raise her arm, very slow, very shaky, and I wonder what she is doing. I keep watching as her arm goes up, slowly, slowly, she reaches something by the window, and pulls and I hear the bell, and aha! I know how to make the bell ring! So I don't get lost this time. And I go home and teach everybody. I gather everybody around and tell them how you have to pull down on cord to make the bell ring and I am so happy that I can help everyone, teach them how not to get lost. That old lady was a good teacher to me."

After Paul mastered the rudiments of urban public transportation, he was determined to make his first American investment. When faced with the vast quantity of American products to choose from, what was the first thing Paul wanted to buy?

"Besides apples?" Paul laughs. "I remember very well what I wanted. I heard about a dictionary, one that would help me learn English words. I would have to go to a bookstore in downtown Dallas to buy it. I asked my mother for some money and she gave me three dollars. I took the bus downtown. Even though I knew about the cord by then, I think I got lost anyway, but I finally found the bookstore. When I found the book, I tried to buy it, but I didn't have enough money. I went all the way back home and asked my mother for more money. She talked it over with my father and he said it was important for me to learn English and that she should give me the money. I remembered her hand was shaking as she handed me a ten dollar bill. It was so much money for us. The next day, I went back and bought that dictionary. Still have it."

A student of American literature and American popular culture might begin jumbling a few themes together to make Paul into the quintessential American Dreamer. First, he arrives in a new land, an innocent Adam in an American garden, then he tastes the fruit of the tree of knowledge, then hungrily goes off in pursuit of an education, to better himself, all the while in the land of the American cowboy, if not exactly Huck Finn's "Territory," at least the Southwestern frontier, the land of power and wealth and J. R. Ewing . . . where a fictional television location—Southfork Ranch—has actually become a successful tourist attraction, suggesting that the *idea* of Dallas, Texas, is more desirable than the city itself.

But Paul isn't familiar with all of those themes. Responding to the American dream, he speaks of a Cambodian dream he once held. "I wanted to be a teacher. I was eleven when the Communists came, when the Khmer Rouge took over. Before that, I was in school. I was a good student." Paul says this shyly, not wanting to appear boastful, and explains, "In Cambodia, you *had* to be a good student. The culture is different. In Cambodia, the teacher can beat you up with a stick. A friend of mine who was forgetful—which was a serious problem since we learn everything by memorizing—got beaten by his teacher, and his parents thought this was good. They thought this meant that he had a good teacher.

"Religion, education, and family are the most important things in our culture. That is why our teachers had so much power. We, the students, all have to wear a uniform and look sharp, have to obey all the time and not talk back. If you have a teacher in your family, your family is high class. Teachers earn a lot of money. And earn a lot of respect. If you see your teacher on the street, anywhere outside of school, you must bow and say *chumriap sua,* good morning, a show of respect. If you don't do this, you just hope your teacher didn't see you. But teachers usually have very good eyes.

"One day, I saw my teacher on the street, but thought he didn't see me, and I didn't say anything. But the next day he asked me, 'Paul, what did you do when you saw me yesterday?' I think, uh-oh. He made me stand in the corner and told me to bring him a stick the next day. I polished it all up so he would like it, and he said it looked pretty good, he would try it out on me. So we are afraid of our teacher and we also love our teacher. Because everything teacher does is for our good."

In a small, fourteen-page booklet, distributed to business, civic, and social service groups, published by the Texas Department of Human Services, entitled "Understanding Cultural Differences—The Indochinese in America," there is a brief section on education. On page eleven, there are four bulleted statements about Education in America followed by their Indochinese counterparts.

AMERICAN:
- Educated people may earn less than less-educated people.
- Educated people do not get automatic respect from others.
- Teachers are not necessarily one of the most respected groups in society.
- Learning the subject is most important.

INDOCHINESE:
- The more educated people are, the higher the salary they receive.
- Educated people are highly respected.
- Teachers are highly respected as symbols of knowledge and learning.
- "Learn good behavior first, then study other disciplines" is a motto followed by the Indochinese.

Seeing the contrasting cultural views summed up so briefly, and so concretely, might be disconcerting. This, too, is a jumble of all those idealized American themes, but a jumble that is upside down, rather than simply mixed-up or confused. If a document such as this pamphlet on cultural differences were to fall into the wrong hands, say those of a seventh- or eighth-grade American-born middle school student, a parent or teacher might be hard pressed to persuade the child of the importance of doing his or her homework, or that good study habits, and the pursuit of high academic goals are at all worthwhile.

Paul's father's whispered definition of "A-mer-i-ca" as the land of freedom and education is one with which most Americans would like to agree. However, if one is to find some truth in the "Understanding Cultural Differences" booklet (and an average of teachers' salaries across the country would provide the proof of at least two of the statements on education), one might conclude that just as the mythical Southfork Ranch represents the *idea* of Dallas better than the city itself, *imagined* America is a much pleasanter place to live.

Paul's boyhood dream of becoming a teacher in Cambodia was one that he kept to himself. Even before the Khmer Rouge made education a capital crime in 1975, Paul did not talk about his education goals. "In our culture, it would sound like bragging for me to say I wanted to be a teacher. That is how highly regarded teachers were. If you said you wanted to teach and you were just from a regular middle class family, your friends would think you were boasting, would ask who you thought you were to believe you could be a teacher."

In America, Paul looked forward to his return to school. Now eighteen years old, he couldn't wait to make up all those missed years of his beloved school. The IRC helped his two older brothers find jobs, then asked Paul what did he want to do. "Go to school!" Paul said eagerly, but the IRC Director shook her head. "She told me I was too old to go to school. I had to get a job, and help my family pay for rent and food. My mother had a job, a hard job in a laundry and my father was disabled from the Communist time in Cambodia, so he couldn't work. It was up to all of us who were old enough to help. The director told me I could go to English as a Second Language (ESL) classes at night, but I had to get a job and she would help me find one."

Paul shakes his head, smiling at the memory of his first job. A member of the Episcopal church found employment for Paul. "I couldn't go to school, but I could clean one. They found me a job as a custodian at Richardson Junior High School."

2

Year Zero

A frog in a well sees the walls around him, the sky above, and he thinks his little well must be the whole world. *Don't you be a frog in a well, Pov.*

—Advice from Paul Thai's father

Although an American observer might appreciate the irony of Paul's situation—his thirst for education not quenched, but whetted by his job mopping up classrooms—Paul's attitude remained optimistic, uncomplaining.

"Here, I am in America, so I am happy. You have to understand where I come from. If you go to Cambodia just one day, you would understand. There, it is death."

Although it wasn't until 1975 when he was eleven years old that the Khmer Rouge entered Cambodia's capital, Phnom Penh and began emptying the major cities and towns, Paul's earliest childhood memories are filled with the sound of shelling, and long breathless nights spent in the bomb shelter. "There was always fighting, always conflict," says Paul. A brief chronology of political developments in Cambodia explains, in part, the constant upheaval.

On November 9, 1953, the Kingdom of Cambodia was established with Prince Norodom Sihanouk as monarch. This ended the control of the French who had made Cambodia a protectorate in 1863. Depending on who is writing the history, Prince Sihanouk is either credited with effectively gaining independence for his country or cynically referred to as a shrewd bargainer, one who convinced the French that he would be easier to deal with than the left-wing dissidents who were starting to make themselves known.

For the next fifteen years, Sihanouk struggled to maintain Cambodia's precarious neutrality. In 1955, Sihanouk gave up the throne in order to become actively involved in politics. He took the title of prince and became prime minister in 1955 and head of state in 1960. From 1955 to 1963, Cambodia received millions of dollars in aid from the United States. In 1963, Prince Sihanouk cut off U.S. aid, charging that the United States supported attempts to overthrow the Cambodian government.

Also in 1963, left-wing opponents of Prince Sihanouk, including Pol Pot, left Phnom Penh for the jungles and mountains. In 1967, Sihanouk's forces crushed a left-wing peasant revolt in the Western Battambang Province.

In March of 1969, the United States began secret bombing in Cambodia aimed at Vietnamese base camps on Cambodian territory. In August of that year, the American-backed General Lon Nol became Prime Minister under Prince Sihanouk, who delegated much of his power to the general.

Exactly one year later, March of 1970, Sihanouk was overthrown in a coup by Lon Nol who allied himself with the Americans. The Kingdom of Cambodia was now named the Khmer Republic. Five days later, Sihanouk, after setting up office in Beijing and denouncing Lon Nol as a traitor, announced the formation of a United Front with his former enemies, those "left-wing dissidents," the Khmer Rouge, to oppose the Lon Nol regime. The next month, April 30, 1970, United States and South Vietnamese troups invaded Cambodia to attack Communist bases. During this period, Cambodia was the target of some of the heaviest aerial bombing in the history of warfare.

Because of the United States and South Vietnamese involvement, the Lon Nol government found itself, at first, fighting the North Vietnamese Army. But over the next few years the Khmer Rouge took over from the North Vietnamese and the fighting on Cambodian soil intensified into a brutal civil war. By 1972, two million Cambodians had been made homeless by the war between Lon Nol and the Khmer Rouge.

On January 27, 1973, the Paris Agreement was signed, ending the Vietnam War, however from February until August, U.S. bombing continued until it was stopped by an act of the U.S. Congress.

On April 17, 1975, Pol Pot's Khmer Rouge took over Cambodia and marched into Phnom Penh. The Khmer Republic became Democratic Kampuchea. Prince Sihanouk was reinstated as the head of state, but was, in effect, only a figurehead, kept under virtual house arrest by Pol Pot's Khmer Rouge forces. In 1976, Sihanouk resigned and Pol Pot became Prime Minister.

For four years, from 1975 until 1979, Cambodians existed in what is now referred to by the survivors as "the Communist time," or "Pol Pot time." For most Americans, it is known as the time of "The Killing Fields."

In 1979, when the Vietnamese invaded, chasing Pol Pot from Phnom Penh and installing a Hanoi-based Communist government, the country became known as the Peoples' Republic of Kampuchea.

In May of 1989, Hun Sen, the Prime Minister installed by the Vietnamese, announced that, in an effort to foster a climate of "national and political reconciliation," the country would now be called the State of Cambodia.

If political machinations, thirst for power, greed, fanaticism, torture, hunger, starvation, and genocide can ever be summed up, capsulized, put in a nutshell, perhaps this will come close: In the last twenty years, Cambodia has had five different names and flown five different flags. In 1975, the Khmer Rouge took over the country which was already ravaged by American bombings and devastated by its own civil war. Pol Pot's reign lasted four years and resulted in the deaths of over one million Cambodians.

For an American to assess this carnage properly, one has to imagine the President of the United States being overthrown. Then the executions would begin . . . the Vice President, the Speaker of the House, the entire House of Representatives, the entire Senate, the Supreme Court, every judge in every lower court, all the college and university presidents, all the teachers, historians, librarians, and the students. Continue to imagine the extermination of all the religious leaders, community leaders, all the property owners, all people who wear glasses, who own books, who have soft hands because they do not do manual labor. Eighty to ninety million Americans.

Cambodian history in a nutshell.

Cambodians themselves do not have the luxury of studying their own history. In their country, the classrooms are in ruins and the only teachers left are the ghosts who moan and whisper through the bombed-out shells.

Those Americans, Australians, Europeans and others who are there to help the Cambodians recover—the church volunteers, the social service workers, the teachers—are hampered in their efforts by the immediacy of other needs: food, clothing, shelter. Because as recently as 1990, Americans would not engage in any trade with Vietnam and Vietnam has controlled Cambodia since 1979, volunteers who set up any type of makeshift school face an absurd shortage of materials. It is not only the books that the Khmer Rouge destroyed that the Cambodians lack. The most rudimentary school supplies—paper and pencils—have been denied to Cambodians.

The Cambodians who have made it to America face stacks of paper—government forms, food stamp applications, leases, contracts. Pens and pencils are plentiful. The irony in this is that most of those refugees who have made it here spent so many years in war and in the camps that any reading and writing skills that they once might have possessed are lost. Any English that they might have learned before the Communist time has been frightened and tortured out of them and any English that they might have been taught in the camps before arriving in the United States sounds so unlike the American English spoken in daily life that there are refugees who question whether or not they are truly in America and whether or not it is really an English-speaking country.

If it is true, as George Santayana said, that those who do not learn from the mistakes of the past are condemned to repeat those same mistakes, Southeast Asians, still reeling from their experiences and denied the intellectual and emotional distancing that learning about what happened might provide, seem particularly doomed.

Americans, on the other hand, do have the luxury and seemingly, the temperament to revel in their past. If the facts and figures, the dates and biographies in history texts are too dry, teachers can capitalize on the current trend in course offerings—nostalgia as history. Well-groomed mothers used to tell their debutante daughters as they coached them in the ins and outs of fashion shopping that they should invest in "good" clothes because those Chanel suits and Italian pumps would never go out of style. Those mothers, thinking no doubt of well-tailored and expensive garments, were more insightful than they ever imagined. Everything comes back according to the fashion writers who predicted the sixties mini and bell-bottom pants as the fashion winners of the nineties. Trendy bell bottoms will probably be the college uniform of choice for those students who pour into classes with names such as "Reading the Sixties," "Rock and Roll Literature," "Mom, Baseball, and Apple Pie—Nostalgia as History," and "American Humor from Benjamin Franklin to Lenny Bruce."

In America, if a fashion, fad, or song lyric remains popular for more than fifteen minutes, we are condemned to repeat it. And if we are not repeating it, we are naming and cataloging it, so that in twenty years we will be able to analyze and codify it or, if it is an object or artifact, collect it. It doesn't take much imagination to envision today's children as the "older" generation, listening to New Kids on the Block and Madonna golden oldies while sorting through their now valuable MacDonald Happy Meal toys. Their children will, perhaps, once again popularize Grandmother's peace symbol earrings.

In the serious-minded worlds of education, business, and politics as well as in the world of popular culture, naming and cataloging have become the primary occupation. Characterizing the American spirit has become the essential task in every discipline. In the classroom, teachers of literature and social studies describe the Rugged Individualist as the quintessential American hero and point to Westward expansion as an American theme. In business schools and boardrooms across the country, the entrepreneur and the CEO vie to embody the American spirit. Along the campaign trail, American politicians explore the New Frontier, stand tall as The Great Society, or twinkle as a thousand points of light.

In pop music, Americans are unrequited lovers or misunderstood teenagers. On television, Americans are exalted as warm, funny, yet sensitive family members and/or tough, streetwise, yet sensitive crimefighters. And in the movies, the American spirit is James Stewart smiling through his tears because he knows "It's a Wonderful Life."

Americans, not particularly famous as mathematicians, can claim "decade-speak"—the characterization of American life for a ten-year period as a peculiar numerical achievement. Despite all the varied and complex events that are layered into each year in a group of ten, no matter the connections to the past ten or hundred or to the future ten or hundred, Americans can condense time into headlines, captions and sound bytes. In the twenties, Americans roared, in the thirties they walked ten miles to school through the snow and pulled themselves up by their bootstraps, in the forties they rationed and riveted and went to war, in the fifties most liked Ike and father knew best. In the sixties, the American spirit was idealistic, in the seventies, self-absorbed, and in the eighties, greedy.

However vain it might be for Americans to find ways to describe themselves and however academic it may be to study American trends and American culture, it has always been part of human nature to attempt to define oneself. Perhaps for America, it is the luxury of youth to allow an identity crisis, a questioning of who am I and what do I want to be when I grow up—America is only a few years past two hundred—and although few individuals actually believe in the concept of a totally assimilated and homogenized populace, America continues stirring the clichéd melting pot of stereotypes, lables and attributes—still cooking, still changing, still growing.

Or perhaps the defining of America truly belongs in the hands of its immigrants since they are closest to the dream and closest to the reality.

Paul Thai, too old to attend school at eighteen, began cleaning Richardson Junior High School in Dallas, Texas, in the fall of 1981. The dream of America as the land of freedom and education—although tempered by the realities of daily life—was as strong as ever in Paul's heart. But Paul was not unaware of the status of his job. "Cleaning . . . being a janitor in Cambodia was the lowest job. It had low pay and low status. So when I found out I was going to be a janitor, I thought, oh no, not that. But I felt like that for just a minute. Because I remembered that I was in America. I told myself that being in America means life and freedom, so I will be happy to be a janitor here."

Although Paul was and is an optimistic individual, his attitude about this first job was less simplistic, less Pollyannaish than it might at first sound. The concept of "face," of personal honor and pride, is vital to the Asian people, and the idea of having to work in a menial position could be quite disturbing. Although Americans often use the expression, "saving face," they are far more adept at recovering from embarrassing situations, and better able to accept their own mistakes or the indiscretions of others than Asians who feel that "face" is not only inextricably linked with honor and with pride, but is also intertwined with their own sense of character and dignity.

Paul's acceptance and philosophical approach to beginning life in America had much to do with where and what he had come from. Paul is quick to remind, "We Cambodians are refugees, not immigrants. We did not emigrate, by choice, to find a better life. We came here to find life, period. Cambodia is death. Here is life." That accounts, in part, for the acceptance of the realities of life as a poor American. In addition, Paul's age plays a part in his attitude.

According to Rebecca Yane, director of the Cambodian Association of Chicago, Cambodians who arrived in America around the ages eighteen to twenty have adjusted better and more rapidly than any other age group. Still young enough and anxious enough to learn American ways, they are also old enough to connect to their families and their past, to the Cambodian culture before Pol Pot time. They quite naturally pay the required respect to their elders while still eagerly adapting to American customs as well. Paul also never lost faith that America could provide him with education, even if pursuing it took a more circuitous path.

The work assignment at the school was not difficult for someone used to sixteen-hour days of manual labor under the supervision of the Khmer Rouge. Paul was assigned to clean twelve classrooms and two bathrooms. Because his workday began after school dismissal, he usually saw no one as he worked. This he remembers as a positive aspect of the job. "I didn't want to see students or teachers while I was doing that job. Sometimes it happened, it couldn't be helped. But I never felt right doing that job with someone watching." Cleaning the classrooms rather than sitting in them and getting the education he so coveted could have been devastating, but Paul discovered that the empty classrooms were empty of students and teachers, not of books.

"I learned to work fast, very fast. I cleaned all my rooms, then I found books that looked interesting and tried to teach myself. I was reading a junior high school grammar textbook that had a lot of conversation in it. When I first looked at the pages, I was kind of lost, but I would pick a word and spell it out to myself and try to pronounce it. I kept a list of words that I found in books, or that I heard again and again, so that when I had enough English, I could ask someone what these words meant.

"I got caught, though. My boss saw that I was reading and studying the books in the classroom and he was worried that I wasn't doing my work. So, he inspected my classrooms, looked all through them and saw that they were clean, all the work was done, and he laughed and said as long as I did my work, I could look at books all I wanted! I began taking the book to him and asking him questions, and he gave me a book, one to take home. It was an English grammar book, so I took it home and tried to study it."

If an American picked up a Cambodian textbook, he or she would see unrecognizable symbols, no A B Cs, but rather   . It would be unlike any familiar system for learning a language. It would be more akin to picking up a decoder ring and puzzling out what each symbol stood for, then trying to put them together in some kind of recognizable form. However, a junior high text would offer few clues, since there are no pictures or illustrations—the study of grammar has never lent itself to visual display—and the sentences used in "high interest" school textbooks are often filled with references to American popular culture that would be as foreign to immigrants and refugees as the words themselves.

This total textbook immersion in English was Paul's earliest struggle with the language, but he soon began taking English as a Second Language (ESL) classes during his time off from work.

"I had an American teacher named Ray Hetzel. My classmates were Cambodian, Laotian, and some Vietnamese. But Ray didn't speak in our languages at all. He spoke only English in class. The first day, I understood maybe twenty percent of what he said. A month later, I understood thirty or forty percent. It got better and better.

"Ray's pronunciation was very good. He would say slowly and clearly, 'What . . . is . . . your . . . name?' And we would repeat and practice. The pronunciation of English words is very difficult for Asian people. Especially the R sound. One time he brought a telephone to class and asked each of us to come up to the front of the room and practice dialing the police to tell them if someone was bothering us. But most of the Asians in the class could not pronounce the word *emergency.* One old woman came up and picked up the phone and didn't dial, just started yelling 'Police, Police' into the phone and we all laughed. We had fun in the class."

Inside the classroom, Paul and the other students were comfortable enough to be at their ease with learning their new language. But the concept of "face" plays a part in an Asian immigrant's willingness to take the risk of communicating with an American outside of the classroom. The difficulty of pronouncing certain words and sounds and the fear of not being understood discourages many from attempting to speak English out in the world.

"I practiced the R sound over and over," remembers Paul. "I couldn't say the word *girl.* I always said 'gul' so I would stand in front of the mirror and twist my tongue and say over and over, 'girrrrl, girrl.' "

Just as an American might marvel at or romanticize the sound of another language, Paul explains that Cambodians love to hear Americans speak English. "English sounds so unique to us. We especially love to hear S sounds. I love to hear an American use the word *systems*! It sounds so good! My brother, Bun, is very good at pronunciation and he does a wonderful Ssss.

"I also love to hear the Thai language. Thai speaking is so soft, so musical, it's as if they are making a tune with their words. It is also completely different from the Khmer language that Cambodians speak. We do not understand each other at all."

There is a common misconception that Cambodians, Laotians, Vietnamese, and Thais have either a common language or languages so closely related that they can easily communicate with each other. Many assume that Asian people have a shared Asian language. Although educated Cambodians from the capital city of Phnom Penh or the few other large cities may have spoken several languages including French and English, those skills were, for the most part, buried in the killing fields. Knowledge of any western languages was a capital offense in Pol Pot time. The Cambodians who came to America in such large numbers in the early 1980s, the survivors, were, for the most part, the uneducated, rural people, whose one and only language is Khmer.

Luckily, for Paul's family that wasn't the case. "Getting translators has always been a problem. I remember that even the caseworker who met our family at the airport did not speak Khmer. He spoke Chinese and Vietnamese. We stared at each other for about fifteen minutes and tried many words before we found communication. My father and mother speak Vietnamese, and three or four dialects of Chinese in addition to Khmer. My mother also speaks Thai. So my parents found a way to communicate with the caseworker, but we children couldn't understand anything."

Although Paul had little confidence in his English during his first few months in America, his ESL classes and his private studies during work at the junior high were helping him progress rapidly. But no amount of classes or textbook pages ever prepares one for the idioms and slang expressions of a language.

"After I had been working at the school for a while, my boss told me that in one of the classrooms, there had been a leak, and there was a lot of water to be mopped up. For some reason, there was a teacher in the room with a few students, doing some extra work or taking a test or something. She motioned for me to come in and go ahead. I never liked anyone to see me doing this work, but she was very friendly, very nice. I could understand a lot of words by this time, but I couldn't believe what she said to me. As I was working, she asked, could she give me a hand? I looked at her and she looked at me. And I thought, this is a nice teacher, but why would she want to give me her hand so I said, *hand*? And she said, yes, give me a hand. This went on for a while, then I finished mopping up the water, never understanding, wishing I could answer correctly."

Native slang would be a difficult problem to tackle when learning any new language, but Cambodians have additional obstacles to overcome in learning American English.

The first obstacle is sarcasm and all of its relatives. Americans often use exaggeration or understatement when they communicate. Or they say the opposite of what they really mean. Paul laughs when he remembers helping an old Cambodian man apply for food stamps: "While we were in the office, I heard one woman ask the woman who was helping us if she was having fun, and this woman was surrounded by papers, and was very mad at us because we were having trouble communicating and she was being very harsh with us and she answered that yes, she was having a lot of fun. I couldn't figure this out. It didn't seem like fun for her . . . or for us."

Another challenge in learning American English is the self-referential manner in which textbooks are written and subjects are taught. A typical exercise in a junior high grammar textbook used in an ESL classroom might ask a student to choose the correct verb in the following sentence: Do you think Gene Hackman is/are a great actor? These kinds of references to popular culture are used in many textbooks to maintain the interest of the student . . . to make the exercises timely and more fun. They place the subject within the context of American culture which can be an added advantage for the ESL student or, in some cases, can be just one more confusing piece of an almost indecipherable puzzle. After all, who is Gene Hackman? A student can learn from the sentence that he is an American actor, a familiar name to moviegoers, but Paul shrugs and shakes his head, "I don't know him yet."

In 1981, when the majority of Southeast Asians began coming into the United States, the school-age Cambodian children had either never attended school in their own country or at least had not attended since 1975 when the Khmer Rouge took power. A twelve-year-old girl would be put into a seventh-grade classroom because it was the age-appropriate grade, but she hadn't been in school since she was six or seven, if she had ever been to school at all. Because she was Asian and Asians have the reputation for being highly intelligent, the teacher would have certain expectations and might unintentionally put a great deal of pressure on her to first catch up with the other students, then excel on her own. The girl would not only be lost in the classroom where English is spoken, she would be unable to understand the chatter, the fashions, the fads, and the manners of her peers outside the classroom. And her parents at home would understand even less, so they would be unable to help her with homework or with her social adjustment. They would only know to punish her if she didn't bring home good grades.

Paul has seen this happen many times. "The American teacher can't communicate with the parents who don't speak English. And in our culture, if an adult such as the teacher speaks through the child or asks the child to translate, the parents are insulted. They might punish the child for interfering in this adult talk. So the child can't really explain things to the parents. Teacher doesn't understand and gives this child who is lost herself a bad grade and tells her to study hard and next time she'll get a better grade, but the child can't communicate this method to the parents, so the parents punish the child. It happens all the time."

Dr. Melinda Cowart, in her seventh-grade ESL classroom at Spence Middle School in Dallas, often refers to popular culture when making a point and she uses a "high interest" seventh-grade text that contains many references to contemporary American life. In a recent lesson on pronoun agreement she asked which was correct: He and I will leave for the movies or Him and me will leave for the movies? When supplied with the correct answer from a student, Dr. Cowart nodded and added that only the Beverly Hillbillies would say him and me. The students laughed and one Hispanic boy nudged his friend and whispered, "Did you hear that, Jethro?"

When asked if she believes that the students understand a reference to a television program such as "The Beverly Hillbillies" and its characters of Jethro, Granny and the rest, Dr. Cowart laughs and says, "They get it because I explain it to them. I always tell them about a show or a reference that I use."

This seems particularly important in today's cable television world where twenty- and thirty-year-old "vintage" television programs are shown along with the 90s "Late Night" and "Twin Peaks." When the channel is switched from the "Donna Reed Show" to "L.A. Law," the changes in fashion, language, customs, and lifestyle of everyday Americans are mind-boggling. If the channel is changed to "The Simpsons," America's favorite dysfunctional family, a cultural family war could break out.

Paul Thai agrees that this combination of words and grammatical rules with the context, with popular cultural references, is essential, particularly for students at a junior high level. "Cambodian parents often encourage their children to watch television. After their homework is done. They hope it will help them learn more and better English." Paul is not familiar with "The Beverly Hillbillies," but remembers his favorite show during his first months in the United States. "I loved to watch the show about the girl who lived in the bottle. 'I Dream of Genie.' We loved that program. It had many things that were interesting for us. There was the magic which we Cambodians liked to watch and also there was the girl herself. She was so silly and funny. In Cambodia, we never saw girls act like that. Or dress like that!"

Television was and is an important part of life for the Cambodian immigrants not only because it offers a chance to listen to the American language, but also because it offers a look into American homes. Despite the fact that most American family units do not resemble the Cleavers of "Leave It to Beaver" or the Huxtables of "The Cosby Show," the new immigrant often accepts them as blueprints of American life.

This is perhaps not so surprising when one realizes that TV families are the only examples of American domestic life that most Asian immigrants encounter. Although Americans visit the Asian homes, as social workers, health care workers or law enforcement officers, the Asians seldom visit American homes or have a chance to observe any type of real American lifestyle. Television is their only means of observation. And it is the simpler, more accessible programs that become favorites . . . situation comedies, soap operas, and cartoons are highly rated by Cambodian TV watchers. One American Baptist minister in Dallas, Charles Morris, recalls seeing small Cambodian boys acting out "The Incredible Hulk." "You'd see these little guys contort their faces and start roaring and throwing their bodies around," he says. "They didn't understand all the words in the show, but they understood becoming the hulk. Then you'd see the little girls spin around three times and become 'Wonder Woman'!"

The children could use their television-inspired fantasies to escape daily life on the streets. Life in "Little Asia/Dallas, Texas" or any other Asian enclave in the heart of a large American city can be as isolated as a remote Cambodian country village. Since most refugees are placed in low rent, badly maintained buildings in the city's worst crime areas and are isolated by both language and culture, they stay within their neighborhoods, often within their own buildings where the youngest children play together in the small enclosed courtyards.

Paul describes the available avenues out of the neighborhoods as school, work, and church. For Paul, the All Saints Episcopal Church, about three miles north of Little Asia, and the New Life Cambodian Baptist Church, located in an old frame house a few blocks from his family's apartment building, became important links to American life. For some Cambodians, conversion from Buddhism to Christianity marks a departure from the Cambodian culture altogether. Conflicts have arisen in some urban Cambodian neighborhood associations over whether Christian Cambodians are still Cambodians at all. The Buddhist Cambodians resist associating with the Christian

Cambodians, but the Christians have much to offer their countrymen and women, since association with the church brings them into closer contact with Americans. This generally means better English language skills and better connections outside the neighborhood.

Paul finds any argument between Buddhist Cambodians and Christian Cambodians somewhat absurd. "I am an American, I am a Christian, and I am a Cambodian. Always a Cambodian. But the Christian pastors are very good, they speak one-on-one with the Cambodians and help us with many problems. When Cambodians arrived here, we had many problems. We still have many problems. Emotional, social, spiritual, financial problems. We had no money, no jobs, no language. Our spirits had been so messed up by the Khmer Rouge, our health was gone. And in those first few years, there were no monks in Dallas. The pastor, visiting door-to-door, offered real help."

Paul, after almost four months of ESL classes, assisted Father Gordon Miltenberger at All Saints Episcopal Church and also became a translator for Charles (Chuck) Morris, his pastor at New Life Cambodian Baptist Church. Paul accompanied Chuck on his round of home visits, visits where they ministered to the needs of the Little Asia community. Chuck remembers Paul as an eager assistant, one who was always there. "Paul, who at that time I knew as Pov Thai, was especially helpful in translating fine concepts, fine thoughts. We could figure out the big needs by ourselves—the need for food and obvious health care needs—but in order to help people emotionally and to find out their backgrounds—where they were from, what their experiences were—in order to counsel them and help them fill out welfare forms and job applications, we needed Pov Thai. And Pov Thai was always there." All of the refugees needed an American friend. Chuck Morris, Father Miltenberger, and the other pastors and assistants could be those friends, and Paul helped everyone understand that.

Charles Kemp, another American friend of Paul's and one of the founders of The East Dallas Health Coalition, the clinic that opened in 1985 to serve the Little Asia neighborhood, also remembers home visits as vital. "As early as 1975, I was aware of Vietnamese refugees in Dallas and wanted to get involved somehow, but when I called refugee agencies, I was rebuffed. They said only church people could go door-to-door and help. I had come home from Vietnam in 1967 and was still trying to figure it all out, so after drifting a while, I went down to Austin and got a master's degree and got involved in hospice.

My wife, Leslie, and I visited Thailand in 1978 and in 1980, but didn't get involved with refugees there. Back here in Dallas, I used to go down to the Little Asia area, just to smell the smells and hear the sounds, because I had good memories of Vietnam as well as bad ones. I kept wanting to do something with the Vietnamese down there, because in Vietnam, I had liked the people I had dealt with on a personal level. So I kept wanting to be involved there. One night, I got together with a doctor of infectious diseases and another woman who was married to a psychiatrist I knew and we went over and did some TB skin tests. My wife and I began working together from then on, going down there, taking people to clinics and to get food stamps, just going door-to-door and introducing ourselves as neighbors, asking if we could help. We did this for about six years and it was very intense. We'd finish down there about 6:30 or 7:00 in the evening and get calls the next morning starting at 6 A.M. Leslie continued with that work and I began sending my community health students into the area in an outreach program and writing grant proposals to get the clinic, The East Dallas Health Coalition, started.

"One of the biggest problems for the Cambodians is that they cannot ask for help. I'm sure there are beggars in every culture, but I myself have never heard of Cambodians asking for help. So if I approach a Cambodian and something hurtful is going on in his life and I don't ask him, specifically, if something hurtful is going on, he won't tell me. So in those early days, we simply knocked on doors and asked, is anybody sick? And there were tremendous problems, a tremendous amount of work to be done, and that's what we did.

"People usually prefer to help others, to interact with them, through a clinic or a storefront, but I think what Leslie and I did, just going through the neighborhood and saying hello, welcome to Texas, our names are ... and we're happy you're here—what can we do to help you? Do you need this, do you need that? That, to me, was more important than anything, any one thing, that we did. Because we were happy to have them here, happy to have them as neighbors.

"I started out trying to do something with the Vietnamese, but as soon as I began making contact with the Cambodians, I realized that it was a different ball game altogether. I mean, the Vietnamese were doing okay. They hurt and they were having difficulty here in the United States, make no mistake about that, but it's comparable to the differences when you triage people. You've got one guy over here who's bleeding and you've got another guy over there with a broken arm—you treat the bleeder first. The trauma for the Cambodians here was so profound, and the pain was and is so profound.

"There was, also, what the Cambodians had to offer. I'll give you this example: If I shoot pool with a really good pool player, I'm going to shoot better pool. Now, if I spend time with these Cambodians, who are really exceptional human beings, then I am going to come out ahead. These are people with unbelievable strength. Because of my work in hospice, I can say this from the perspective of someone who has spent a lot of time with people who were dying, who were staring death, staring eternity in the face, and there were strong people there, so I know something about people in extreme situations. And the Cambodians were unbelievable to me. They have this grace. And *grace* is the appropriate word here, I think, to help me understand who they are. They have tremendous grace in lives filled with pain. Because, you know, everybody smiles and everybody's pretty and nobody is complaining . . . and then you get to know someone and things begin coming out. A woman will say about her children, 'Sleep, sleep, die.' And you know that's the way people die of starvation. Consciousness ebbs away and they die. *Sleep, sleep, die.* And so we've taken the deaths of these children she loved and put it down into three words. She's not going on about it and I'm not going on about it, but there it is. There's little understanding of language between us—my wife and I have been together twenty years and we often have trouble understanding each other—but here, it's a different language, a different culture, so it strips away a lot of excess, a lot of meaninglessness. You're left with essence.

"There are those here with incredible stories. And they're not telling it all. There are stories that they will never tell. You can put together a lot from what one tells you and another tells you who was at the same place, the same camp at the same time. You can piece stories together. But there are a lot of secrets and some secrets are better left untold.

"The Cambodians lost all their leaders. They got the head of their culture chopped off. Their spiritual leaders were killed, their political leaders were killed, their military leaders were killed. The implications of that are profound. For the Jews . . . well, the Nazis did not discriminate—everybody had to die. But the difference for the Jews—and I know the people who survived the camps might have something to say about this, but, at least to some extent, world Jewry was waiting. Some of the people from the camps feel bitter about their reception, but the Hebrew Immigration Service was waiting. And there were learned men and women in the camps who survived. This was not the same for the Khmer. The Vietnamese, as corrupt as their leadership was and is, came over intact. The Vietnamese had a great number of leaders who came to the United States and stayed. It was different for the Khmer. Some of their best leaders had a chance to leave, but chose to stay. And they ended up in the killing fields. At a time when the Khmer people needed God more than ever—and I know God is everywhere and all that, but most of us need a little help—there were no monks in Dallas, no spiritual care. Sometimes a monk would come up from Houston or some other city, but the first monk to come and live in Dallas didn't arrive until 1985.

"There is tremendous dissonance here. What is prized in their culture is not prized in ours. For example, I encourage my son to ask questions, to speak up, but in the traditional Khmer home children do not interact with the adults. They don't rush in and say, daddy, daddy, who's this, what's that? At least they didn't do that before, but now, in America, they are beginning to do that. So there is this enormous adjustment for people who are already dealing with crushing grief. There are differences in how people interpret things, but the Khmer people love their children just as much as we do, even if they express it differently. I remember one time, General Westmoreland was on television talking about Asians and how they don't value life as we do, and the camera cut over to a Vietnamese widow who was crying about her husband's lost life like any other widow.

"Everyone's lost kids or parents or brothers or sisters or someone real close and there is all this unresolved grief. It's as if everyone has somebody who is MIA. They don't know if they are dead or suffering or living two blocks over on the next street. Nobody knows.

"We went through one thing here where we couldn't get apartment owners to put in the right kind of mailboxes, so the mail would deadhead and end up back down at the main post office. Now a white boy could go down and get his mail, but the Cambodians couldn't because they didn't have IDs with their pictures on them. So they couldn't get their letters. Incredible grief and frustration.

"The grief and the frustration add up to incredible pain. And this pain isn't valued by Americans. I don't know of any other word to use except *valued*. It's not appreciated. You hear these stories . . . everyone knows someone who was on the helicopter where a woman left her kid and took the pig instead or something like that—absolute rot! Everybody wants to believe something about the other guy, in this case, the Cambodians. But my experience is—and I really pay attention to what is going on—there is tremendous love and grief, tremendous loyalty. And sacrifice for family. You know some people have faced this issue—you're a mother and you've got three children and you haven't got enough food. So who goes hungry? Who's got to die? It can't be you, because if you die, all three kids die. So it's got to be the smallest, the weakest, whatever. So people make this decision. And live with it all the rest of their lives. And they do. You can go on for hours about all the losses and everyone who was lost, but in the end it all adds up to pain. And with the Cambodians, you see this strength with their pain.

"People use the word *survivors,* but that doesn't seem like quite the right word. The pain, the strength bring me back to the word *grace.* There is tremendous grace in the way they have gone on. I've worked in psychiatry and I know people have their secrets and that people aren't nice all the time. I don't have any illusions that these people are superior beings. But I know strength when I see it. And I know power. And I see it here."

Paul Thai shakes his head at the power Charles Kemp sees *here* and remembers the power he faced *there.*

"Back in 1975, when the Khmer Rouge took control, they wanted to start everything over," Paul explains. "They wanted to start at Year Zero. They wanted everything to be under *Angka. Angka* means government, but it's a new way of government. They believed that the past was full of corruption, that the government had sucked the blood of the people, thought that the rich had been bad to the poor. They wanted to start something new—*Angka.* So they started sending letters, telegrams to Cambodians who were out of the country studying. They asked the students to come home and start rebuilding their country. And when the students came back, guess what? They ended up in the killing fields. Their bones are there."

Year Zero. Starting from scratch.

"So Angka starts Year Zero and looks for people who worked for the government, students, rich people, people who wore glasses, people with high foreheads, people with short haircuts, people with soft hands, people with sharp fingernails, people with light skin. Those people with light skin are classified as rich people, and I am considered light-skinned, my whole family is light-skinned because we have some Chinese ancestors, so we are considered rich. And these are the people that Angka wants to get rid of. Angka believes that if these people are allowed to live, they will be the ones that rebel against Angka. They will be the ones who want the old way, not the Communist way. This is just one example of how the Communist way is different.

"Under the Communist, if I have a relative who lives in another town, maybe thirty miles away, I cannot just travel to see him. I must request a passport to go visit. I must request permission from Angka. If I do not ask permission, I will get no coupon for food. I will starve to death. So Angka doesn't want people who might rebel against their way. So because Angka is beginning a new way, Year Zero, they line people up in the killing fields. They line them up all the time. This I have seen with my own eyes."

Paul Thai, now twenty-six, describes what he saw "with his own eyes" when he was twelve years old.

"When my uncle, my uncle's whole family . . . his children, my aunt . . . were taken to the killing fields, I followed them. I hid and watched. I saw what they did to my uncle. They didn't use guns because they were afraid to waste bullets. So they killed my uncle and aunt, my cousins, with a stick. They beat them to death. And they buried them with hundreds of other people. It was just one big grave."

And what was Paul's uncle's crime against Angka?

"They said he had a big mouth. You see, one night, at a teaching session that they call a meeting, they ask if we love Angka and my uncle said, 'Yeah, we love Angka, but we are so hungry that we can't serve so well, can't work so hard.' He said that if we had enough to eat that we could love our Angka even more. That is why he and his whole family had to die."

This violence against their own was not what Paul Thai and millions of other Cambodians thought would happen when the Khmer Rouge marched into the cities in April of 1975.

The country had fallen, but that meant that the corruption of the Lon Nol government, the oppression of the poor by soldiers and government officials, the elaborate systems of bribery devised to keep the poor poor and the rich rich—those evils would fall, too. And for those who believed in Prince Sihanouk, both as a political and spiritual leader, his promised return meant a new life for Cambodia.

"When the country fell," Paul remembers, "we thought we were free. We thought that those soldiers were our saviors."

Families bustled about, preparing food, cooking special dishes for the

Khmer Rouge soldiers who had marched through their towns. Paul shakes his head when he says, "Even our family had given the Khmer Rouge food."

But in the following days, after the announcement that the Lon Nol regime had fallen, the Khmer Rouge, wearing black and speaking into large microphones, marched into Phnom Penh. They announced that everyone must leave the city within twenty-four hours. They gave a specific reason for the immediate evacuation—Americans were going to be dropping bombs. Over loud speakers, they promised that everyone could return after twenty-four hours, either to stay or to return to other cities and villages that were also being evacuated. The people were commanded to hurry and told that they should not worry about their belongings since they would be returning in a day or so to reclaim their property.

At this time, the Thais lived in the small city of Poipet in western Cambodia. Before 1970, the family had enjoyed a middle-class life in Phnom Penh. Paul's father owned restaurants, his mother cooked, and the rest of the family helped run the business. But the civil unrest and destruction that had taken its toll on the country had taken its toll on the family as well. Ill-mannered, often violent soldiers who frequented the restaurant and refused to pay bills drove out paying customers which eventually drove the family out of business and farther away from urban comforts. Their first home after Phnom Penh was Kirirom, west of the capital city where Paul's father tried the restaurant business again. When he found himself wrestling the same problems that had plagued him in Phnom Penh, he moved the family away from city life altogether. In Poipet the family was living in relative poverty, gardening and raising a few animals for food and a meager income.

On the day the Khmer Rouge marched into town, Paul was in school at the temple where he had been studying with the monks for three-and-one-half years. When he heard that he was to return to his family, he remembers having mixed feelings. "To be honest, I cried a little bit when I had to say good-bye to my master. He had taught me so much. I was so used to him, his words, his stories. He had bought me my bowl and my clothes to be a monk. I was going to be a monk myself in about three weeks. I was just a child so I didn't know it was good-bye forever, but I knew I would miss him no matter how long we were going to be separated."

At home, the Thai family packed. "Just some clothes," says Paul. "We expected to come back." The family left their house and joined their neighbors in the streets.

"I had a dog when we left. My family raised pigs, chickens, ducks, and when we left Poipet, we had to leave them all behind. But my dog followed along behind us. I felt stupid, but I cried for my dog then. I just loved that little dog. When I would come home from the school for a visit, my dog would run to the fence and lick me all over and I would hug him like he was my baby brother. I didn't care much about leaving other things behind, but my dog, running along behind for about a mile, made me sad. We called him Kiki which is a common name for a dog in Cambodia, but his real name was Keno. It took me a few weeks before I could forget about him." Paul's eyes make it clear that he has forgotten little about his past, but has put away certain sorrows, exchanged them for greater grief. An American might say that he and his countrymen and women have been forced to put things in perspective.

Thousands of people clogged the roads. The Khmer Rouge soldiers had ordered the people to go into the countryside, telling them that would be the safest place for them now. No one was allowed to stop. "After five or six hours, we wanted to stop to rest, but the soldiers would not let us. They warned us that the bombs were coming. We had to keep moving." Paul remembers that his family and the rest of the people moved day and night. They were allowed to stop for only a few hours in a twenty-four hour period. This went on for four or five days.

Paul explains how quickly and how certainly the peoples' image of the Khmer Rouge soldiers changed:

"The soldiers kept telling us to go fast and we saw them beat people who slowed down. In one place, we heard the soldiers ordering a woman to pack and go. She refused and said she couldn't go without her baby and her husband who was too sick to leave. The soldiers called her a bitch and said that Angka said she had to obey. She cried and said that in the future she would do whatever Angka wanted, but not this time. Then we heard the lady scream. Then we heard the shot that killed her. We saw the baby roll out from her arms. We saw the soldier stab the baby with a bayonet. Then we heard another shot. They killed the husband. So we knew then that the soldiers were not our saviors."

When Paul's family reached a village near the Laotian border called Kontrey, meaning "Little Fish," they wanted to remain. Other families were also allowed to stop there. They knew no one there, but as they sheltered under a tree, the village leader approached them, brought them food, and offered to let them stay in a barn.

But the Khmer Rouge were taking over the villages, setting down the rules and regulations.

As they went about *reorganizing* the country, Khmer Rouge soldiers constantly investigated families. Not only did they ask the children to tell them about their parents, their parents' occupations, family friends and personal business, they actually hid under houses to listen in on families who thought they were alone with each other.

Fathers warned their children not to say anything. And since families who stayed together could draw a certain strength and support from each other, the Khmer Rouge needed to isolate them.

Fathers, mothers, and children were separated and sent to labor camps or concentration camps. Paul's father was sent to a concentration camp, his brothers and sister to various labor camps and his mother, after some time in a labor camp, was returned to the village to work and care for his baby brother.

"Even my five-year-old sister had to work," remembers Paul. "Her job was to collect the bull droppings to use as a fertilizer.

"All the time we worked. Day and night. We were not allowed to talk because we might say something against Angka. And during this time when we were in the labor camps, the Yotears (Communist soldiers) kept searching for people who used to work in the government.

"My group of thirteen-year-olds was building dams. So we worked all day, building the dam to hold back the water, but the water kept building, too, so we had to work all night, staying awake to make sure the water didn't overflow, because if the water overflowed, it would kill our plantation. So we worked ten to fourteen hours in the daytime, then had one meal of watery rice, then stayed awake all night. Then, when we finished one dam, they would move us to another location and we would start all over again, building another dam, day and night. Also every night, they called a meeting. And if we weren't at work building and watching, we had to go to meeting. I call their meetings brainwashing.

"Every night, they talked about Angka. Angka this. Angka that. They asked if we loved our Angka. They told us that they wanted to build a new country and that we kids were the future of Angka, the future of the country. So they said, 'Tell us if your father used to work for the government. Tell us if someone you know doesn't like Angka, your uncle, your cousins . . . and we will get rid of them for you. If you love your Angka, do whatever Angka says.' And I said to myself, 'God, you think we are stupid or something?' but they started to earn the trust of some of the kids. The kids started saying, 'Yeah, my father used to be a soldier,' or 'Yeah, my father owned a motorcycle,' or 'My father owned land.'

"I was so scared that time. My father had owned two restaurants and he had a lot of soldier friends. My mother had worked as a cook at the restaurants, my older brothers had been waiters. And I thought to myself, am I going to tell them about my family? Am I going to let them kill my family?

"But, somehow at that time, I do love Angka, too. Rebuild a new country? I love that idea! My brain was being washed. They talked about the corruption of the old government all the time. And it was true that with the old government, poor people died every day, so I thought, maybe this is true. Maybe rebuilding our country is a good idea.

"Somewhere in my mind, though, something said, 'No. Don't tell them anything about your family.' So I listened to the others and when I heard a kid say his family used to be farmers, I heard the Yotears say that this was good. It was considered good if you were a farmer because it meant that you were poor. I could see that they weren't going to do anything to the kids whose families were farmers.

"They made us take turns. They went to every kid and asked what his father did. Kids were saying, 'Yeah, my father was a teacher,' or 'Yeah, my father was a doctor.' And when it was my turn, I said, 'My father? I'm sorry, but he was a farmer, real poor, we didn't even have a house to live in.' And they asked me how I could be a farmer, how come I have light skin? And I told them I didn't know, but that I was a farmer and I knew how to plant rice. But believe me, I had no idea how to plant rice. I didn't even know how to lift a hoe."

Haing Ngor, in his book, *A Cambodian Odyssey,* says that he was pleased and thrilled to win the Academy Award as best supporting actor for his portrayal of photographer Dith Pran in the film *The Killing Fields,* but that he knew his best acting performances were over before he escaped from Cambodia.

Paul remembers someone who unwittingly supported him in his performance before the soldiers. Another boy whose skin was even lighter spoke up that he was a farmer, too. "And he really was a farmer, they knew that, so that convinced them that I could be a farmer even with my light skin. So I was saved that time. My family was not taken away."

In addition to the direct, visceral horrors of daily life in the labor camp—the beatings, the starvation, the slave-labor working conditions—there were other invisible tortures to be endured. One of Paul's friends, an eleven-year-old boy, decided he could no longer endure the loneliness of being separated from his family.

"We had been in camp together two, two-and-a-half years. He was a few years younger than I was. He cried every single night because he missed his parents. I cried, too, and I missed my parents, but I didn't want to do anything to make the soldiers mad at my family. But this boy wanted to run away to the village to see his parents. He wanted me to come and I told him no. He said he didn't care what happened, but that he had to see his family. He left in the night. It took him at least a day running to get back to his village. But when he got back to his mother's house, a soldier was waiting for him. Somehow they knew and got there before him. He never even got to see his family. They brought him back to camp and hung him right in front of everybody. The soldiers said this was an example of what would happen if you tried to escape from camp. They said, 'Angka is your family now. And this boy, instead of showing his love for Angka, tried to escape. This is what happens if you try to escape. Angka loves you, but Angka has to teach you a lesson, too.' So this boy hung there half the day, then they took him away. I believe they took him to the killing field. I don't know.

"The camp was soldiers everywhere. A bell rang and you worked. Everywhere soldiers were watching you. And you worked rain or shine. No good shelter. If you got sick, you didn't get fed—food had to be earned. There was another bell for a meal, but it was just a bowl of watery rice. They gave us twenty minutes to eat that, but we were done in a split second. Then the bell rang to go back to work. There was no medical care—if you got sick, you stayed in camp, you didn't get fed. You got well alone or you died.

"I never saw one sympathetic soldier.

"Before the Communist time, I had never seen a dead body. Or someone beaten to death. The first time I saw a bloody body, I passed out. The second time, I had a headache and my heart beat faster, but I didn't black out. You get used to it, but it's never good, it's never okay.

"The soldiers declared no love, no family. They said that there was no time for love or for family, because we had to use all our time to serve Angka. Once they caught a man and woman about twenty to twenty-five years old making love. The called a big meeting of thousands of people, and hung the couple in front of them. Then they stabbed them. People did not want to watch. I did not want to watch. The Yotears pointed guns at us and said we must watch. That was my second time watching people getting stabbed."

The Khmer Rouge used young children as overseers of the workers in the camps. "While we worked, these little kids who had been brainwashed would watch us. Then, when the day was over, they'd single people out, say they didn't work hard enough, point out that their hands were not dirty enough. The soldiers would drag off the ones pointed out by the children and suffocate them by putting a bag over their heads."

In the villages and in the labor camps, radios were not allowed. Despite the blackout on news, information, and even conversation, rumors somehow managed to be whispered. In 1979, Paul and his fellow workers heard that a Khmer Rouge leader had left their area because he had heard that the Vietnamese were coming.

"We were still working, though, because the Yotears were still over us. Then we started hearing bombs about a mile away. The Khmer Rouge were getting scared. The next day, the bomb sounds got closer and closer. Then the soldiers left—they said, 'You stay, we're going to go check with Angka.' Then we saw Green Soldiers. We thought they were Cambodian freedom fighters, we didn't even know they were Vietnamese. We clapped our hands and cheered, then saw many soldiers in big trucks and people in the fields started running away from them. We figured we would try to run home. There were thousands running, every which way. I just followed some of the other kids because I didn't know the way anymore. After running about six or seven hours, I got to my village.

"I saw my mother and my little sister and brother, but not my father. My mother said that he was working in the garden where he had been sent. She told me to run and get him. It took about two hours. While I was running there, I saw people running everywhere, every direction, soldiers, too.

"When I got there, my father was still working. I told him that everyone was running away, that the freedom soldiers were there to help us. He acted like a man in shock. He asked if I was kidding him.

"I tried to pull him, to drag him but he couldn't run. He had no weight, just bones, no flesh. He couldn't run, but could only walk very slowly. I held his arm and we got back to the village after about four hours. When we got back, everyone in my family was there except for one older brother who worked in the city, not the village. We waited for him.

"Everyone said to leave the village because the Khmer Rouge would come back, but we were not going to be separated again. Only one other family, our neighbors, stayed in the village that night along with us.

"It was so quiet that night in the village—only the two families. And there were no other noises—it was as if the dogs and chickens and birds knew that it was Communist time and they shouldn't make noise."

3
He Called Me Mr. Thai

Thus not only does democracy make every man forget his ancestors, but it hides his descendants and separates his contemporaries from him; it throws him back forever on himself alone and threatens in the end to confine him entirely within the solitude of his own heart.

—Alexis de Tocqueville, *Democracy in America*

Father Chuck Morris says that the Asians want three things after they settle in America . . . first a car, then a television, then a stereo. He says that is their measurement of status. Paul agrees that these are the most desirable objects, but emphasizes that they have less to do with status than with survival. "We have to work here in America. That is the most important thing . . . to get money to pay our rent. My father understood the concept of rent because he had rented the restaurant that the family operated in Cambodia, but for most Southeast Asian people, *rent* was something entirely new. People in Cambodia built their own houses and lived in them. There was an independence in that. Now, arriving here, Cambodians are told immediately by their sponsor, their caseworker that they must get a job to pay rent and buy food. So, the Cambodians look around at the Little Asia neighborhood where they're placed and don't see a lot of opportunities for employment. They find out about jobs, about workplaces, and they need transportation, so they try to get a car as soon as possible. Many families pool their money to buy cars, sometimes terrible cars that don't run very well if they run at all, so that they can all ride to work together.

"But they need something else besides the car to take them to their jobs. They need to be able to understand, to speak to their employer, in order to get the jobs in the first place. And the television and stereo, the programs and the radio and the music all help with language. This is how the Cambodians find out about how to act, how to talk, how to get along with the Americans. There are many Americans who want to help the Cambodians, who come into the community to visit and ask about health, and talk about social services that are available. They come to see us. But we Cambodians don't have very many chances to go and visit American homes. We would like to know what American homes look like, how American families act. The television helps us learn about the American culture. My wife, Marina, watches some of the soap operas that are on in the afternoon. She loves "One Life to Live" and "General Hospital." She says that they teach her about how Americans act, how they dress, and what their homes, their lives are like. And there are good stories to follow. These programs are her opportunity to visit Americans. So the car and the TV and the stereo are not just status symbols, they are tools. They are the tools for survival in America."

During Paul's first year in the United States, there were small, ordinary pleasures to counterbalance the daily realities of earning money and the difficulties of being so frequently lost in the language and customs of Dallas, Texas, America. Paul developed a taste for fast food and often carried out hamburgers and French fries from McDonald's. No manual on cultural differences explained to him, though, that he did not have to stand in line with the cars, yell his order into the speaker, walk around to windows one and two, and pick up his food order to go. Observation and embarrassment were his teachers for that lesson.

Trying to fit into the contemporary fashion scene presented some embarassing problems as well. When Paul and his family arrived in America, their caseworker took them to a church basement where they could pick out some clothes. There were agencies that provided funds for new winter coats and shoes for refugees, but this was a steamy Texas summer, and the family needed to choose some things for everyday wear.

"We came with nothing, so anything was better than nothing, right?" shrugs Paul. "But there were some problems. These used clothes that were donated . . . they were American-sized clothes, not Asian-sized! We were smaller than most Americans anyway, but especially when we first arrived. We were so skinny that it was very hard to find pants that would fit us! I felt lucky because I did find a few things. Some pants, some shirts. I remember that I was very excited to find some plaid pants! They looked so special that I planned to save them to wear for the New Year celebration!"

Most Americans who, when cleaning their closets, load up bags with outdated dresses, pants with spent elastic waistbands, coffee-stained sweaters, threadbare jackets, and drop them off at their churches or local Goodwill or Salvation Army stores, collecting a receipt on the way out to use for tax deduction purposes, know very well the kinds of clothes that Paul and the other refugees had to choose from—clothes that, given a choice, no American-born American would wear.

Comedians and television writers have exploited the dress of non-Americans in America for years. Comedians Steve Martin and Dan Ackroyd drove audiences into a frenzy with their parody of two "wild and crazy guys" from Eastern Europe, dressed in outrageously loud tight pants and wildly printed, mismatched shirts. Amy Tan, in her bestselling autobiographical novel, *The Joy Luck Club,* writes of a child remembering with embarassment her Chinese mother's inordinate fondness for the "wrong" pastel colors for winter clothes. Magazine articles that focus on immigrants regularly feature photographs of smiling men and women dressed in a zany mix of discarded designer shirts, stretched-out knits and oversized bell-bottom pants. This sad uniform sends several messages to potential American employers as well as to potential American friends. For an adolescent who arrives at junior high school or high school in this fashion, the message is likely to be "stay away—I not only look different . . . I dress funny," and for adolescents, this can easily be the kiss of social death. For the adults, whose skills, intelligence, and talents have to be judged in order for them to get the jobs they so badly need, it is vital to find Americans who can look beyond the clothes and see the individual.

Paul is realistic but philosophical about his first American clothes. "Now when I look back on the pictures we have from those times, I realize how funny we looked—wearing all those clothes that were out of style. And wearing them the wrong way! When I first put on an old suit that had a vest, I wore the tie on the outside . . . I was so proud to be wearing an American suit—I didn't know that the tie was supposed to be tucked in. So we have all these photographs of me in a suit with my tie hanging out looking so dumb!"

Conquering fashion is a negligible problem compared to facing the other cultural differences between Americans and Southeast Asians—Cambodians, in particular. The majority of Cambodians who arrived in the states in the early 1980s were people used to rural life. In Cambodia, families built their own homes. Over ninety percent of the country practiced the Buddhist faith. Each handmade house would have a small altar with a statue of Buddha, candles, a bowl for offerings, and some incense. Outside, the family kept a few animals if they could afford them, and tended a small vegetable garden. Most villages had a marketplace where people bought and sold goods, but more importantly, where they visited with each other and socialized.

The strong Buddhist faith held people together through a system of belief and a code of behavior. There was a respect for family that came before all else. In the Buddhist way, family and education came first. In addition to the philosophical and religious arguments that might exist between Cambodians who have remained Buddhist and Cambodians who have converted to Christianity, Paul feels that the major cause for disagreement lies in their different views of family. "In Christianity, the faith comes first. Even though you are supposed to honor father and mother, it is belief in God that comes first," explains Paul. "But in Buddhism, family comes first. There is a story that the monks told us in school about a woman who wanted to be very good, wanted to pay great respect to her ancestors in the Buddhist way. She brought all the best food to the monks and spent all her time at the temple honoring her ancestors. Then the monks asked her what she did for her own parents at home, the ones who were still living? She couldn't answer because she was not paying them respect, not taking care of them. They told her to go home and honor her own family.

"Many Cambodian parents worry about their children becoming Christian, becoming Americanized. They think it means that they will not honor them when they are old. Traditionally, Cambodians have taken care of their own families, taken care of the old parents, in their own homes. There are no nursing homes or old people's homes in our culture. We have always felt that our parents took care of us when we were small and helpless and we should pay them back by taking care of them when they become old and helpless. We honor age. It is a compliment in our culture to tell someone he is old. It means he is wise and worthy of respect.

"I know that I have a young-looking face, but I am not complimented when someone calls me a boy or says I look young. To me, that is an insult. When I was a child in school at the temple with the monks, I was called *Acha* which means elder. I was just a child, but the monk who was training me trusted me and taught me all the responsibilities of the *Acha,* the elder who assists the monks. Since we had no one older there to serve as *Acha,* I did it, and it was a great honor."

The American emphasis on youth, the drive to be fit, to have a young body, a young face is in direct opposition to the respect paid to age in the Cambodian culture. "The television commercials for health clubs with movie stars and singers who talk about having young bodies seem very odd to us," says Paul. "We think it is good when people look like they get plenty of food to eat."

The relationship between children and adults is another area in which cultural differences run deep. In a Cambodian family, the children do not speak out in the presence of adults. They are expected to be disciplined, quiet and respectful . . . speaking only when spoken to. When houseguests arrive, children are expected to greet them, be introduced, then be dismissed. And when parents are making family decisions, they do not seek the opinions of their children.

"You can imagine the problems for Cambodian families who have grand-parents that believe in the old traditional ways, parents who were raised in the old way but have learned some of the American ways, and now there are the children who, through school and television, are very, very American!" Paul shakes his head as he tells one story from the Little Asia community.

"A young Cambodian girl was walking down the street, holding hands with a Cambodian boy. This is very much against our culture. Boys and girls, men and women, do not show affection in public. But this girl's parents saw her with this boy. They were upset and angry. She told them that he was just her friend, that it didn't mean anything serious. But the parents insisted that because there had been such a public display, the girl had to marry this boy. She protested that she did not love him, he was just a friend, but the parents were the authority in this and they ordered marriage.

"The boy didn't mind because he liked this girl a lot. His parents met with the other parents and the marriage was arranged. The boy's family agreed to pay the bride's family, which is custom, and the wedding was planned.

"But after the wedding came the wedding night. The boy said it was time to go to bed and the girl said no. She liked him as her friend, but she did not want to go to bed with him. He was very angry and went to her parents to demand the money back that he had paid them.

"The parents were very angry and they beat their daughter. This kind of punishment, physical punishment, is common in the Cambodian culture. And this daughter, their daughter, had caused her parents much embarassment. She had disobeyed them, disgraced them. They had lost face because of her. The girl ended up in the hospital emergency room.

"I was called in to translate so I heard the whole story and it is a very sad one. The parents were acting like normal, good Cambodian parents, but in America, they were being accused of child abuse. In Cambodia, child abuse does not exist. Corporal punishment is acceptable. That doesn't mean, though, that Cambodians are always beating their children. Children are taught to respect their elders, to obey. They are trained to have self-control and self-discipline. Cambodian family life is very difficult to duplicate in America. The rules and customs are so different. And this girl, whose parents beat her so badly, was following the American way of individual freedom, individual choice."

Although a social worker was called in on this case, and the girl did not immediately go back to live with her family, she and her parents did eventually reconcile. In 1989, by her choice, she married again . . . in a traditional Cambodian wedding ceremony.

The clash between old and new and the marriage between old and new are constantly taking place in Little Asia. Paul describes young teenage Cambodian girls walking home from school, wearing makeup, jewelry, and chattering with their friends. "As they get closer to their home, they take off their makeup and get quieter and quieter, so by the time they end up at their families' doors, their heads are bowed and they give a respectful greeting to their parents before going off to do their homework."

The booklet mentioned earlier, "Understanding Cultural Differences," describes in the section entitled, Dating, some pertinent opposites of American and Cambodian social customs:

AMERICAN:
- A woman can go out unchaperoned with a man.
- Men and women can visit each other at their respective homes or apartments.
- Two unmarried members of the opposite sex can share an apartment.
- Sex is discussed openly.

INDOCHINESE:
- Generally, a woman does not go out alone. Groups of men and women may go out, but rarely alone.
- Depending on the relationship, the woman generally won't go to the man's house until they are engaged.

- Two unmarried people of the opposite sex sharing an apartment is extremely rare. This usually means the couple has a common law marriage, and even then it is frowned upon.
- Sex is not discussed openly.

Paul saw his wife, Marina, for the first time in 1982. They did not speak directly to each other nor did they allow their eyes to meet and linger for the first several times they met. Paul laughs about this, "I was a good Cambodian boy, and," he adds, "I was just a kid so I was scared."

Marina Miech was a traditional Cambodian dancer. Because so many Cambodians who attended the All Saints Episcopal Church missed seeing the slow, subtle movements of the traditional dance, and because the church pastors were conscientiously trying to help the Cambodians retain their cultural heritage, Father Gordon Miltenberger sought out dancers and musicians from the community.

A Cambodian named Son Hang played the *tro,* a traditional stringed instrument. Others who played the *tro* and drum agreed to play and a small band was formed. As a kind of uniform, the church had blue T-shirts made, lettered in both English and Khmer.

When the musicians were found, Marina and some of her girl friends who knew the traditional dances agreed to come and perform at the church. Father Miltenberger asked Paul if he would ride with American graduate student, John Macucci, who was a volunteer in the Little Asia community. John would drive his car to pick up the dancers and Paul was to come along and translate for them if necessary and assist them in any way he could.

Paul agreed to help, as he always did—no minister or community worker ever remembers Paul saying no. Paul is modest about his active role as translator for the church and as a volunteer community worker. Charles Morris of the New Life Cambodian Baptist Church characterizes Paul as having "the heart of a servant," and as being one who could never say no to anyone in need. Paul shrugs this off and says simply that he has always liked to help his people.

But Paul says that helping the dancers was a different kind of volunteer task. "After I saw Marina, I said that I am the only one that is going to help them! The only one that is going to pick them up and give them assistance!

"I didn't drive myself then, but I went with John every time to pick up all the girls and bring them to the place where they could rehearse. I looked at Marina as often as I could, and I thought I noticed she was looking at me, but we didn't talk. We could not talk because we hadn't been introduced by an adult.

"The dancers were very popular. After they danced at the church, there were schools that invited them to come and dance. So the girls wanted to rehearse more as they performed more. So I would pick them up and take them wherever they needed to go. Sometimes when Marina was dancing, she looked at me and I got such a good feeling. I loved it. So I thought she knew that I liked her and I began to think that she liked me.

"In the car, going from place to place, she would say something to John, who was older, about her family or about her home, something that she wanted me to know. And I would do the same. We couldn't communicate directly, but we could let each other know things about our lives.

"Then Marina got sick with the mumps. Even though I was helping out a lot in the church, my English was really not very good then. So we took her to a Vietnamese doctor who had a Cambodian translator. They are the ones who sent her to the hospital in Garland. So John and I took her to the hospital and went there to help her, to visit her and that is how I got to know her mother. Her mother asked me if I would bring her to visit her daughter and I agreed. Then, the second time I took her, she asked us to stop at a store so she could buy something for Marina. Then she looked at me and said, 'Aren't you going to buy something for Marina?' and I said, 'Sure, sure.' My mother had given me about five dollars, so I bought a lot of chocolate bars to give her. She ate them when I gave them to her, to please me, but I found out later that she didn't like them. So that time, after I visited, I left my phone number and told her to call me if I could help her in any way. She called me later that night after I got home and we talked for about an hour. After she got out of the hospital, I began visiting her and her family and she came and visited me, and after about two years, we got married."

Dating is not the only topic pertaining to romance that is outlined in the "Understanding Cultural Differences" handout. There is also a short section on Showing Affection:

AMERICAN:

- It is more acceptable for women family members to hug and kiss than male family members and friends.
- It is not uncommon for a man and woman to hold hands, hug, or kiss in public.
- Parents and children of any age can hug and kiss in public.

INDOCHINESE:

- Members of the same sex can touch.
- Overt displays of affection by men and women in public are not acceptable.
- A father can touch and hug his daughter when she is young (ten years or younger), and a mother can touch her son when he is ten or younger. However, the father will avoid touching his daughter and a mother will avoid touching her son after they are ten years old.

Paul remembers walking down the street in Dallas with his good friend John Lim. They had been friends since their days together in Khao I Dang camp. "We were walking and talking with our arms around each other and people kept whistling at us. Men would roll down their car windows and holler and whistle and I thought something must be wrong. I am not that good looking!" Paul laughs.

An American friend explained the differences in customs, then explained the term "gay" to Paul who remembers being embarassed. "In our culture, men together is not commonly accepted at all! I told my friend that we would have to remember to follow the American custom at all times!"

Paul also remembers with some amusement that a parent in the Little Asia community told him that their son said he preferred to rent and view American movies over the Chinese movies that are popular and readily available in the neighborhood. "Because," the son told his father, "there is kissing in them. I love American kissing!"

"It's true," says Paul, "that in a Chinese movie, even if a couple is very much in love and they have been separated for years and years, when they get together, they will just say hello and maybe shake hands or bow or something. In an American movie, if a couple is separated for a few minutes, they come back and hug and kiss. And they always say, out loud, in public places, I love you, I love you!"

Paul's father warned him against those words, *I love you,* as part of his parental advice to Paul on the subject of marriage. "My father said I should never tell Marina that I love her because then she would have that power over me. He said that once a wife knows that her husband loves her, she will stop being a good wife, and will lose respect. That is something I don't believe. On this subject, I like the American way. I am trying very hard to learn to say, I love you."

It is not only direct communication between husband and wife that is difficult for Cambodians. Paul explains that all direct communication is difficult for Asian people. Americans value "telling it like it is" and "spilling their guts" while Asians value silence and tact. Paul sees a need for Asians to give more American-type voice to their feelings.

"In the Cambodian way, if a friend of mine says something or does something to offend me, for example," says Paul, "I would not tell him about it. I would just stop being his friend. Even if it was my best, closest friend, I would just silently stop considering him my best and closest friend. He wouldn't even know why. I think the American way on this is better. We should talk things out. I see Americans talk and argue then afterwards, they are friends again. Back to normal. I think this is a better system."

A sad example of this Cambodian internalization of emotions was illustrated in the aftermath of a tragedy. In Stockton, California, a madman opened fire on the Cleveland Elementary schoolyard, killing five children, then himself. Four of the children were Cambodian. The fifth victim was Vietnamese. Psychiatric counselors who specialized in trauma were called in to work with the schoolchildren, their teachers and their parents. They were stymied, however, in their efforts to help the Cambodian families. Not only did the grieving parents refuse outside help—they were completely mystified as to why social workers and psychiatrists continually asked them how they felt. As health-care worker Charles Kemp has pointed out repeatedly to the groups he addresses in Dallas and other communities, "The Cambodians deal with their enormous pain in silence . . . with a kind of unbelievable strength and grace."

For Americans, therapy, both individual and group, has become a commonly accepted part of daily life. Analysis is no longer for only the seriously mentally ill, clinically depressed, or extremely affluent. Even television programs such as "The Bob Newhart Show" or "Dear John" have successfully used the analyst-patient or group analysis premise for situation comedy.

Therapy and its variations exist in several forms . . . rap groups, consciousness-raising groups, support groups, codependency workshops, self-awareness seminars, and racks upon racks of self-help paperbacks. For those who lack the get up and go to get out and make an appointment or for those who cannot afford the price of the latest "How-to," there are a myriad of radio and television shows where guests and audience members share their deepest secrets and "talk out" their most private problems. Viewers are even encouraged to share the experience by calling in and telling their own stories.

Paul remembers being horrified the first time he saw the "Oprah Winfrey Show." "People were talking about very personal subjects. Husbands talking about their wives and wives talking about their husbands. People were discussing private family problems. I only saw it once, but I could not believe my ears and eyes!"

It is not only the personal revelations to strangers that are shocking and dissonant to the Cambodian ear, but also the personal comments made between friends and spouses. "I never told Marina that she looked beautiful. In the Cambodian culture, that would not really be a compliment. If I told her she was beautiful, she might think I was just admiring her body, not thinking of her as a whole person," says Paul, "and she would be insulted. She would think I was making fun of her.

"You see, here is the thing: Since I was born, since I was a human being, I have never heard my mother or father say, 'Paul, I love you.' I never heard my teacher say, 'Paul, I love you.' We just don't express ourselves with the word *love* that much. Boyfriends and girlfriends do not use that word."

Love is a universal language, though, and according to movies, television, song lyrics, and greeting cards, love transcends words—it shows in actions and expressions. Although Paul and Marina did not use the word out loud, Marina's mother, to use an American expression, saw the writing on the wall.

"Because I was visiting at Marina's house a lot and she was coming over to my house to visit, and because we often met at church, rumors began to spread about us. One day, Marina's mother called me to her house.

"She said she had heard a lot about me and her daughter, and she wanted to know what I was thinking. I loved Marina so much then, but I said to her mother that we were just friends. And her mother said I didn't have to play like that with her, so I admitted that we loved each other. Then she asked about marriage.

"I said that I was sure she wanted her daughter to go to school and that we should wait, but she said that we could not wait if we were in love. It is not like we were being forced to marry, but in our culture, our parents believe that if we love each other, we should marry before we are tempted to do something we shouldn't do before marriage. You see, it is not acceptable for couples to go to bed together before marriage and parents fear their children might do just that if they wait too long for marriage. So Marina's mother said that we should marry as soon as we could.

"I went home and begged my parents. My father understood, but he was very mad. He told me that he thought I was such a smart boy, the smartest boy, and he wanted me to go to school. He wanted me to go to school forever, I think, because his whole idea of America was that it meant education. Because he thought I was smart and because he knew that I always wanted to go to school, he believed I was a hope for the family's future. He didn't want me to be married, he wanted me to go to school."

At that time, in early 1984, marriage and school seemed as if they were either/or options. Paul was now working as a printer's helper and knew nothing about night school, or extension classes, or GED. He assumed that when he got married, he would continue to work, and his dream of education in America would remain a dream. Marriage meant working, making a home for his wife, and raising children. School did not appear to be in the picture.

Paul and Marina married on March 17, 1984. Theirs was a traditional Cambodian wedding. They wore formal Cambodian wedding clothes that they rented for the ceremony. Both the bride's and groom's costumes were ornate and finely crafted, worn only on this special occasion when a man and woman are to be dressed and treated as a king and queen. Both the bride and groom wear makeup on their wedding day, another custom that signifies the importance, the special nature of their roles on this day.

Paul's wedding was Buddhist, a traditional Cambodian wedding. How is this reconciled with his conversion to Christianity? "For us, the wedding is part of the Cambodian culture. It is important to have the monk come, or the *Acha,* the elder who represents the monk. He might be wearing a suit and not a robe—this is America, not Cambodia, but it is important that he be there. We follow the Cambodian way in our wedding because we are Cambodian. This is our culture. It doesn't affect our religious beliefs.

"It is important for us to dress as the king and queen, to make this day special. When I entered the house, my brothers held an umbrella over my head. The sun was not supposed to shine on me. I was supposed to remain fresh. I couldn't enter the room until Marina met me with a bowl of water and washed my feet. She only pretended to do this, as a symbolic gesture, to show that I would now be her leader, the leader of the family." Paul shakes his head ruefully and emphasizes in an American fashion that this leader business is indeed symbolic.

"Then I could come in. And as the *Acha* meditated and blessed our marriage, he prayed for the magic comb and the magic scissor. And as a symbolic gesture, they cut our hair, just a little, so it would grow new, together. After the ceremony, we fed each other banana, for strength. And at the reception, we brought cigarettes around to the guests and lit them for them. This, too, is symbolic. It shows that we want to serve our guests, to thank them for coming to bless our marriage."

To understand how the Cambodian wedding remains Buddhist, yet more culturally Cambodian than related to religion, it might be necessary to consider the American wedding . . . of any religious denomination. There is perhaps no other ritual in American society that has remained so unchanged through the years. Vows may be rewritten, and music and fashions may change with each season, but weddings seem to cling tenaciously to custom.

It is not even difficult to find the American counterparts to the Cambodian wedding traditions and symbols. The renting of formal clothes for the groom, and in many cases, the handing down or borrowing of the bridal dress from mother to daughter . . . the importance of appearance for both bride and groom on their special day. There is the feeding of wedding cake to each other as a sweet and nourishing gesture that seems closely related to the Cambodian feeding of fruit. It is true that few American brides today would consider performing even a symbolic footwashing, and yet the custom of a father handing over his daughter to the groom, the use of a veil in traditional wedding dress, and even the superstitions that surround the bride being kept out of the groom's sight before the wedding all hearken back to ancient traditional roles of men and women, parents and children, husbands and wives . . . and have been slow to change as compared to other customs that have vanished with the changing American consciousness.

Even the Cambodian custom of offering cigarettes seems familiar. Before the majority of Americans began thanking others for not smoking, it was unthinkable not to have matches inscribed with the bridal couple's name and wedding date placed at every table at the wedding reception.

Finding similarities in customs, in the exercise of American and Cambodian rituals, might interest Americans. It delights Paul. "If an American were dropped in the middle of China and didn't know the language or any of the customs, he or she would look for someone who spoke their language, who followed their customs, someone who could translate for them," Paul reminds. And translation doesn't always involve words found in a dictionary. "I ate a hamburger at a fast food restaurant and it tasted so good! I didn't know what it was or how it was made or anything about it . . . it was totally new and strange to me. So I spent hours looking for 'Whataburger' in the dictionary! That's why it's nice to hear when things are the same or see things that are the same in the American culture."

Paul learned that one significant difference in the wedding customs of Americans and Cambodians is that of the honeymoon. In Cambodian culture, it is traditional that the newly married couple go to stay with the bride's family for three days and nights. Paul learned from Larry Munoz, his boss at John A. Williams, Printer, that this was not the typical American honeymoon.

"Larry said that Marina and I should go away by ourselves, on a honeymoon, and not stay with my mother-in-law and the rest of Marina's family. That sounded pretty good to me, but I knew we had to follow the Cambodian custom," says Paul. "Then Larry gives me this surprise. He collected money at work and paid for a three-day stay at the Marriot Hotel for Marina and me! He told me it was already paid for and he couldn't get his money back so we had to go and stay there.

"This was a hard decision. So we worked it out like this. The first night we stayed with Marina's family. That is what she wanted and it would have been an insult to the family if we had not come. I was so uncomfortable, though. I was a very shy, quiet boy, and when I came out of our bedroom, I had to sit with her family and they would try to make conversation with me. I was not good at that kind of talk, the small talk. I remember especially that Marina's sister was always trying to get me to talk to her!

"But the second day, we went to the Marriott Hotel. I explained to Marina and to her family that the money would all be lost if we didn't use this gift of the weekend in the hotel, so I persuaded everyone that this is what we should do . . . so that we would lose only the money for that first night.

"The hotel room was nice. I liked it there. But Marina didn't like it. She cried because she missed her mother, missed her family—she was used to having people around."

The newlyweds stayed only one night at the Marriott, then returned to Marina's house.

After the first three days of being a married couple, Paul, twenty-one, and Marina, nineteen, moved in with Paul's family. This, too, is the Cambodian way, however the two-bedroom apartment in Dallas was far more crowded than their house in Cambodia would have been. Paul's parents slept in one bedroom, Paul and Marina took the other one. All of Paul's unmarried brothers and his sister slept in the small living room.

Soon after Paul married, an American friend at church told him about GED. "I had given up on thinking about school, but when I heard this, that I could get GED, and that it would mean I could continue my education, I said, Yeah, I'll do it." Working long hours at John A. Williams and studying for the GED did not leave many hours for leisure. Any weekend time that might have been spent with his new wife or exploring the city or visiting with family and friends was usually taken by those who needed Paul's skills as a translator.

"People called me at all hours," Paul says. "Actually, they still do. The ministers from the church would call and ask me to go on home visits with them. You see, many people would just smile and say they were okay, even when we knew they were not. Maybe they couldn't get their check cashed or figure out how to open their mailbox or maybe they didn't have enough food to eat. I enjoyed helping the people in my community. I always still enjoy it. There was—is—always something to do for people who are newer in America or who don't understand as well. I liked being able to show people the American way of things.

"One of the jobs I always had was taking people to the doctor. Or taking them to the hospital or clinic. The worst was when I had to take the pregnant women. On Saturdays, I would take all the pregnant women who had appointments for their checkups at Parkland hospital. I remember one time I had to take seven pregnant women! People would give me such funny looks. And we would get there and wait. And wait and wait for each appointment. It would take all day. And I would get home really late and Marina would be waiting for me. Sometimes not so happy with me, I think."

If Marina was indeed unhappy about Paul spending his Saturdays with several pregnant women, it may have been because of her own condition at the time. Marina and Paul married in March and expected their first child nine months later in December. Paul, working and volunteering in the community didn't have any time to spare, but managed to make the time for childbirth classes. "I was there when Chetra, my son, was born. We had natural childbirth," says Paul proudly. "In Cambodia, in a small village like where my family lived, the baby would be born at home. The midwife would come and take care of the mother. The Cambodian word for giving birth means 'to cross over the water.' After the baby is born, the mother is isolated from the rest of the family and a fire is built under her bed, to keep her very, very warm. Not very safe, maybe, sometimes the mother gets burned from the fire. But if all goes well, goes correctly, then the mother and child will be okay, will cross over safely.

"My son, Chet, and my daughter, Maly, born later in June, 1986, were both born in the hospital and I was there for both births. I was happy to be there. But in some families, the mothers will give birth at home, then call the doctor or the hospital. They feel strongly about the old way, that the baby should be born at home."

The Little Asia neighborhood had no parks, no playgrounds with park benches for Marina and other young mothers to sit together with their strollers and compare notes on their children's development. The kind of loose, informal support group that often rises spontaneously in middle-class neighborhoods was absent in Little Asia. That is true, in part, because of the close and private Cambodian family unit. Grandparents and older family members are often living in the same household or at least nearby so they help the young family learn how to cope with babies and young children. If Marina had a question about Chetra's development, the way he crawled or formed his first words, she had many willing and capable advisors. Paul's mother, in particular, loved watching her grandchildren now that nurturing children was once again a happy and hopeful task.

Another reason, though, that the neighborhood streets remained so empty of women and children during the day was the high incidence of crime in the area. The Asian residents, Vietnamese and Laotian as well as Cambodian, were easy prey—unfamiliar with language and customs, often lost or confused about their location, and characteristically slow to report violations against them and their families . . . if they reported them at all. Police in their uniforms, officials of the government, enforcers of laws were too reminiscent of the Asians' recent past. Where Paul and his family had come from, people in uniforms took people away—usually forever. Another fear that prevented the Asians from reporting crime or asking for help was their worry that they should not cause trouble or ask for help. If they were too much trouble, wouldn't America ask them to leave?

Because Paul did so much work for the church, transporting people to hospital and clinic appointments and taking neighbors to apply for their food stamps and welfare, the ministers helped him to buy his first car, a 1977 Ford Grenada. "It was beige," remembers Paul, "and it broke down every week." Paul's brother had taught him to drive in a large paved vacant lot on Pecos Street, across from the IRC Welcome House, the house where Paul's family spent their first nights in America. Paul says that the lot is where most refugees learn to drive. "All the time, you see Asian people going around and around in circles here."

Paul remembered that the police officer who came to investigate his family's stolen television set was respectful to his father, but he was still fearful when he saw a police car, red light flashing, signalling him to pull over. "When I saw the red flashing light, I thought, uh-oh, I am going to die in America now.' But the police officer was not what I expected. He was friendly and asked for my name. I told him it was Pov Thai, and he said to me, 'Mr. Thai, you were driving without your headlights on.' It took me a few minutes to understand what he meant because I was so surprised. He had called me *Mr. Thai!* He wrote me a ticket that cost thirty dollars which is a lot of money. But at that time, I was so happy, I didn't care about the money. He treated me as an individual and paid me respect. All that mattered was that he called me *Mr.* Thai."

Paul's first photograph. Someone snapped this shot of Paul (right) and another boy at Khao I Dang. Paul says they posed hand-on-hip because they thought they should try to look tough and serious.

Paul, fourth from left, poses with other boys from the Transit Center. This was taken three days before he came to the United States.

Paul, kneeling left front, poses with other residents of Mairut Camp.

Paul is baptized at Transit Center. The missionaries provided one-on-one counseling for the refugees who desperately needed physical, emotional, and spiritual attention.

A Christian party in the refugee camp. Paul is in the back row, third from left. Those who smiled in the photos were often the ones who already knew they were leaving.

In Dallas, July, 1981, Paul models his first American suit. No one told him that the tie was supposed to be worn inside the vest. Hands are still on hips, the pose is still meant to be cool and tough.

Paul's father and mother and brothers and sister in their first American home, a one-bedroom apartment in Little Asia, Dallas, Texas.

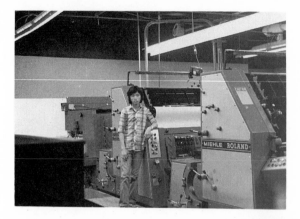

Paul stands by one of the machines at the John A. Williams Printing Company. Loading paper, assisting at the press, was his second job in America.

Paul poses with Marina soon after they met. This was a secret photo because neither of their families would have allowed them to be photographed together after only a few day's acquaintance.

On Paul's wedding day, March 17, 1984, he is escorted by friends and family and shielded by an umbrella to keep him fresh.

Paul and Marina, in traditional Cambodian costumes, exchange their wedding vows. The Buddhist *Acha* or elder is officiating.

As part of the wedding ritual, Marina feeds Paul a banana to nourish him and give him strength.

At the East Dallas Storefront, Paul talks with a resident of Little Asia. Above his head is the Cambodian flag that pictures the temple at Ankor. Next to it is the flag of the Dallas Cambodian Lion's Club—the first Cambodian Lion's Club in the United States.

This sign above a drinking fountain in another public building in the Little Asia neighborhood illustrates the diversity of the community residents. Signs printed in five or more languages are not unusual here.

The East Dallas
Storefront (Credit:
Catherine Rooney).

Corporal Ronald E.
Cowart at his desk
at the storefront.
His corner was
filled with paintings
that graphically
depicted the killing
fields of Cambodia
and photographs of
the refugees who
called Little
Asia/Dallas home
(Credit: Sharon
Fiffer).

Paul, in his PSO
uniform, helps a
caller with
translation (Credit:
Sharon Fiffer).

Paul is flanked by
fellow police
officers Thao Dam
and Leck Keovilay.

4

Two Escapes

It was a custom in Cambodia that people would come to the monks with an offering and ask them to predict a lucky number for the lottery. One night, when I was a student at the temple, I had a wonderful dream. A beautiful traditional Cambodian dancer who looked just like Marina—even though I didn't know Marina then—gave me a lucky number. In the morning when I woke up, I remembered the number and my family played it and won. I don't remember how much money, but it seemed like a lot. I told my master and he was mad at me—he said I should have told him the number so he could give it out when the people came with their offerings.

—Paul Thai, describing his dream

In the dead of that silent Cambodian night, when even the rooster and chickens were fearful and mute, Paul's father wordlessly awakened the family. Each listened . . . father, mother, Mao, Muy, Bun, Chi, Pheap, Chandy, Many, and Paul, who at that time was still called by his family nickname, Pov. They heard footsteps, someone running, soldiers running. Many, only three years old, began to cry. His father silenced him with his hand. The other children were shaking. They heard someone crawling in front of the house. Paul remembers thinking as the door to the house slowly opened, now we are going to die.

The family sitting rigidly still in total blackness heard a whisper.

"Mommy, Daddy, are you there? It's me, Tang Thai." Paul's fourth oldest brother had returned to the last place the family had called their home. It was a miraculous reunion, but as Paul points out about all the survivor families, there was always so much luck, so many miracles in staying alive. Unlike a jubilant happy-ending scene, the Thai family's joy, relief could not be celebrated. They still could not make noise. The footsteps, the running sounds they had heard were all real. Soldiers, undoubtedly Khmer Rouge, were rummaging through the village.

Paul's father gathered them and made them sneak quietly out of the house and into the garden. Hiding in the shrubs, among the vegetables, they heard someone approach. Paul's father raised the stick he had picked up as a makeshift weapon. But again, the whisper was a friendly one. It was the father of the neighboring family who had also stayed that night, waiting for a returning son.

"Brother, we have got to leave here. Right now. It's not safe," he whispered to Paul's father.

Both families crept to a house on the edge of the village and hid under it until dawn. In daylight, the Vietnamese soldiers returned, and the Khmer Rouge who had prowled through the town at night disappeared. Some protection, a shred of confidence by day and chaotic fear by night became the normal pattern for the Thai family and their countrymen and women. This pattern would continue. The families gathered together only essentials—what food they could find, a pan for cooking rice, anything they thought might be useful for trading, for buying food, and moved on. They didn't have a destination. No one had even mentioned Thailand. They just moved away from the old village, in the direction that the crowd was going.

"We followed the crowd to a county called Serey Sophorn. We stayed there for about two months. We had to go to fields far away to harvest rice. The Vietnamese were trying to win us over as we went back near the village to get the rice and find vegetables. The Vietnamese were protecting us," Paul says, then adds, "by day."

Dead bodies were everywhere. The fields yielded death as the major crop. Soldiers, Khmer Rouge, Vietnamese, farmers, peasants, innocent families caught in the crossfire. And victims of disease, starvation fell into the same mass graves left undug and uncovered by the Pol Pot soldiers. Paul remembers seeing people try to bury some of their friends, but they would be in such a hurry, they could only cover one half of the body. The other half would be sticking out above the earth.

"You see, the Vietnamese were only with us during the day. At night, they were afraid of the Khmer Rouge, too, so everyone hurried. During the light, everyone had to work hard to find food." And if there was time, to bury the dead? "Yes," says Paul, "if there was time. But everyone was always tired, weak, sick, too. There was not enough food to eat and we couldn't sleep at night. One night we were right in the middle of the Khmer Rouge and the Vietnamese fighting, so we hid in the river. We stayed there the entire night, in water up to our necks. My father held my little brother above the water. All night."

What options were open to Paul and his family, free to starve during the day and caught in deadly crossfire at night? There were no safe havens, no jobs. There was no rebuilding. Weakened by the physical and mental horrors of Pol Pot time, few Cambodians had energy to think beyond the next few grains of rice that would serve as a family meal. People were displaced, on unfamiliar ground and the leaders, scholars, and spiritual advisors who might have inspired them were under their feet, buried throughout the countryside.

Paul, at fifteen, took up the occupation of the day.

"I became a smuggler. In 1979, when the Vietnamese took over, starvation became the major cause of death. We didn't have any food. No one had any food. So I walked from where we stayed into Thailand to buy stuff and bring it back to sell. It usually took from two days to a week each way."

When asked about the legality or illegality of smuggling in 1979 Cambodia, Paul thinks for a moment and shakes his head.

"I don't think it was illegal, I mean not really in the way we would think of it here and now. Everybody did it. But legal or illegal, it was dangerous. The Thai soldiers could shoot you any time they wanted.

"I couldn't believe one thing that I saw. You see, to be a smuggler you had one or two big bags with you all the time and a stick so you could balance the bags on the ends of it and carry the stick on your shoulder. This one man that I saw had one small piece of a diamond, a very small diamond, and showed it to a high-ranking Thai officer who was carrying a pistol. The officer nodded and said, 'Ah, good,' and pulled out his pistol and shot the man right in the forehead. The man fell down and his bags went flying off in either direction. Then he got up. He got up and was having convulsions, but he was looking for his bag and pole. He found it, picked up everything and got it together, and then fell down and died.

"And I thought, this could happen to me. We were smugglers and we had to earn food for our families. Watching this man get up and gather his things together said to me that he was still trying to feed his family—even as he was dying—he was trying to get his things together to give his family. I cried at this."

As amazing as it might be to witness someone with a bullet in his head get his belongings together, the wonderment is not so much that the man did not immediately die, but that he could will himself to live. In America where most, although not all, have enough food, and most, although not all, have shelter, employment, and the freedom and independence that come with a measure of success, the will to live is more easily understood. In America, even if things are bad, they might get better. Despite the bureaucracy, the red tape, the daily hassles and indignities one in need might have to face, the United States does have resources, does have social service programs, agencies, sympathetic individuals. The Cambodian smuggler with the bullet in his brain had little hope that his life and living conditions would improve—some might even say that he should welcome death—but that will to live, to go on providing for the family, burned inside of him.

Remembering the murdered smuggler, Paul shakes his head. "I knew it could happen to me."

The guns of the Thai soldiers were only one of the occupational hazards of smugglers. The paths through the jungles were mined and booby trapped. "If you got lost or lost track of the people ahead of you on the path, you just stayed there," Paul explains. "When I was with my brothers, sometimes we would lose sight of someone leading ahead, so we would just wait there. Sometimes we would stand there in the jungle for four or five hours, waiting for someone who knew the path better than we did. Then we followed.

"We bought food mostly, sugar and rice. Some bought tobacco. But the number one thing was sugar! People were so skinny. They all wanted sugar to eat. We also bought a lot of clothing at that time from Thailand. Shirts or pants that would cost two dollars in Thailand were sold in Cambodia for ten dollars. So we would often trade clothes for rice.

"It was hard for my mother, waiting for us to come home. Sometimes, if we got separated from the others, my brothers and I would take so much longer to get home, maybe two weeks, and my mother would be at home, praying and meditating and wishing for us to come back." Paul adds, "With the stuff."

Paul's mother spoke Thai and, before 1975, had herself made many buying and selling trips between Thailand and Cambodia. After the Communist time, her migraine headaches became so severe that she could not make the frequent trips. "It was hard for her to send us," Paul says, "but it was necessary."

Paul's family began seeing more and more people moving west. "My father talked to our neighbors and asked where everyone was going, walking from east to west, and the people said they were going to Thailand, going near the border, then they were all going to escape from Cambodia. The Vietnamese soldiers who were in our country didn't care, but the Pol Pot soldiers, the Khmer Rouge, didn't want us to leave. If we even talked about wanting to leave, they would consider us traitors to our country."

Paul's father felt that this was the first step toward America and packed up the family to leave Serey Sophorn. They joined the foot traffic moving west and they, along with the other travelers, were attacked again and again by Thai robbers.

"We saw women raped by the Thai robbers along the way. In front of their families, in front of everyone. The robbers would come up and demand money or gold and if you said that you didn't have anything, they would kill you. So we gave them everything along the way. We had so little. It was hard for us to believe—the Khmer Rouge were so bad and now the Thai robbers were so bad."

"It took us two days and two nights to get to the Thai border. When we got there, we didn't stay in a city or a town, but in the forest. It was the rainy season and we had no shelter. We slept under a tree, but the tree didn't help much when it rained. And," Paul adds, "then there were the mosquitoes."

When Paul's family arrived at the border, they found no formally organized camps. Later, as more and more Cambodians moved west toward the border, they were traveling along on rumors of camps, settlements with names and the hope-filled promise that they would see and feel the presence and protection of Americans and Europeans when they reached their destination. But in the early days, the camps came into being when enough Cambodians arrived in one place and stopped. That stopping place was the camp—in the middle of nowhere, with no food or shelter. The first camp that Paul's family came to was called by its residents Nong Chan.

"Then the American Red Cross came to us. They gave us some tuna fish, some rice, and pots and pans. And they gave each of us one piece of plastic. We hung our plastic on a tree for shelter. When the wind blew, we still got wet, but it was better." Paul says simply, "The American Red Cross saved our lives."

The number of Cambodians who camped along the border where Paul's family had stopped increased. Paul estimates that a few hundred families grew quickly to a few thousand families. Nong Chan grew daily, as did the other settlements along the Thai border, until June of 1979, when Thai soldiers came and spoke to the Nong Chan refugees over a large microphone. "They always used a big microphone," Paul remembers.

The Thai soldiers made the announcement over their loudspeaker that the Cambodian refugees had been waiting to hear. They told them that the time had come to leave for America. "You are all going to America. We have buses to take you. Pack all your things. Take all your valuables."

"We were so happy and excited!" says Paul. "My family was the first one on the bus! Everyone was yelling and signing that we were going to America. We rode the bus for two days. When we stopped, it was dark, maybe around midnight, and the soldiers told us to get off the bus and find a place to sleep, then they would be back in the morning to take us to America. We really believed then that we were on a bus ride to America.

"In the morning, I thought I was dreaming as I woke up. I thought it was a dream that everyone was moaning and crying. But I opened my eyes and found that it was no dream. Even my mother was crying. I asked her why she wasn't happy, after all, weren't we going to America? She couldn't talk, she just pointed her finger straight out.

"Then I looked around. I saw where we were. On top of a mountain, in the Dangrek Mountains. There are two mountains there, like twins, that are named this because they look like the pole and bags that are carried by the peddler or the smuggler. On the side of the mountain we were on was Thailand and on the other side was Cambodia. And it was considered impossible for anyone to get off this mountain. Then I cried, too."

The Thai soldiers returned to the weeping Cambodians and robbed them. The soldiers ripped away the last hidden valuables, the pathetic treasures, the precious grains of rice and the few broken pieces of jewelry that had been saved or scrounged for this trip to America. Then they told them to go back to Cambodia. On foot. Down the mountain.

Some of the refugees, out of their minds with grief and fear, began running. Paul remembers seeing some of them, seventy-five to one hundred of them, shot in the back as they ran toward Thailand. After making their point, the soldiers told the others to start running, this time toward Cambodia, and began shooting to hurry them along down the mountain to almost certain death.

"We were all separated," Paul remembers. "We were running around, wild, because we didn't know how to get down the mountain and mines started blowing up. The whole place was mined and booby trapped. I could hear the mines and I could hear the screams. I heard people yelling to their old parents, 'Mother, Father, you are going to die up here. I can't get you down, I'm sorry.' The parents understood and told them to go ahead.

"A lot of women left babies up on the mountain. Everywhere you saw the babies, heard them crying. Many babies and many elderly, many sick people were crying. Their families left them.

"One woman, she refused to leave her baby. She wanted to take that baby. She had it only two or three weeks, that's how young the baby was. She made it to the bottom of the mountain with us. It took one day and one night. And when we got to the bottom of the mountain, we still had to walk slowly, because there were so many mines. At the bottom, I found my parents and my brothers and sister. My second brother, Muy, was wounded, but not too badly. So many others were wounded, hurt. Some had lost legs, lost half their bodies from the mines, but kept on moving. Some were screaming. I remember hearing many screams for water, but we couldn't get anybody water because there wasn't any water, not even for ourselves.

"Walking through the jungle was very slow. No one wanted to walk in front. No one wanted to be the one to step on the mine. So we would all move forward, inching along, then someone at the front would feel like their luck was about over and would go no further and someone else would have to lead the way. I was walking near the front. The woman who had refused to give up her baby was walking ahead of me. She stepped on a mine. She heard the click and screamed for everyone to get away from her because when she moved again, it was going to blow up. But she begged for someone to come and take the baby. She had made it all the way down the mountain with the baby and now she knew she was going to die, but said she would die happy if someone would just come and take the baby from her. Finally, after a long time, one man stepped forward and said he would. Then I don't know what happened, maybe she got excited or anxious, but she must have moved, because the mine blew. We never even found her body. But we saw the baby's head.

"I felt terrible. I know everyone felt terrible. But the whole way, the whole time, we had to step over bodies. We went on this way through the jungle for thirty days and thirty nights. Sometimes we would just go one half of a mile in a day because fear of mines would make us go so slowly. We would just sit down. We would try to find things to eat. Roots, bark of tree, bamboo shoots, anything that didn't look poisonous. We would eat and have to go to the bathroom and sleep all close together. No shame, no more shyness between us, between boys and girls, we just all stick together.

"After the thirty days, we got back to Serey Sophorn where we had come from before. It's near the west already, but we had come from the east, from the mountain and jungle and it had taken us so long. Out of the jungle, back in Cambodia, we walked probably another four or five days getting back to the village."

It is now estimated that nearly forty-five thousand Cambodians were taken by buses into the Dangrek Mountains and abandoned. It is impossible to know for certain how many thousands died there.

Paul's family settled back into village life, such as it was. The same lack of food, goods, employment, the same fears and life as pawns between the Vietnamese and the Khmer Rouge soldiers prevailed, but it was at least familiar. Paul remembers that he and his mother both said, "Cambodia is our home and we are going to stay here."

After two or three months, though, Paul's father gathered them together. "I still want to go to America," he told them.

Paul remembers the family meeting. "My mother said, 'Hey, say that again, please? America? Don't you remember what we've been through? Do you remember the jungle for two days and two nights getting there? And do you remember the mountain? And do you remember the jungle for thirty days and thirty nights?' And my father said, 'Yes, I remember. But I want my children to have freedom and education. I don't care if we die along the way.'"

Paul and his mother and older brothers all said no. "No more, no more! Especially my brother, Muy, who had been wounded, he did not want to go again. We all agreed that we would not go. But the next day, my father gathered us together again. And he talked. And talked and talked and talked. He began to convince us that we had no future in Cambodia. He made us realize we were all going to die sometime anyway, maybe sooner in Cambodia rather than later in America. So we started becoming convinced. He gave us the courage we needed. My mother said no for a long time. Then my father lied to her and said if she didn't come, we would leave her there alone, so he convinced her that way. We all came over to his way of thinking, except my brother, Muy, who had been hurt on the mountain. He refused to come with us. He is still in Cambodia. We lost him there for many years. We wrote and sent his picture and tried to get information, but could not locate him."

(Eleven years later, Paul's family did find out that Muy was living just outside Phnom Penh with his family. A Cambodian neighbor of Paul's father went back for a visit, found Muy, and videotaped him giving a message to his family. Paul shakes his head, saying, "He looks very old to me now.")

"So again, we go the same way, take the same route. Two days and two nights through the jungle. Then we come to the border, but we stay on the Cambodian side this time. There are thousands of people there. We begin our smuggling again—sneaking into Thailand to buy stuff and bring it back to sell—still black market. Same products—sugar, rice, tobacco, food, especially fish like sardines."

The thousands of refugees who camped on the Thai–Cambodian border were not only devastated by poverty and hunger. They found themselves once again, against their will, in the middle of a war zone. "The Khmer Rouge were fighting the Vietnamese and the Cambodian freedom fighters were fighting both groups. So there were three sides to begin with. But the freedom fighters were divided, they didn't get along and had two separate groups with two different leaders. So four groups were constantly fighting.

"No one could ever sleep. And then there were the Thai soldiers. I remember one time a high-ranking Thai soldier came into our camp in the daytime and he raped a Cambodian woman. A Cambodian freedom fighter came in and found out about it and got so mad that he shot that Thai officer dead. Other Thai soldiers came and got the body and took it back, then they decided the Cambodians had to pay for their soldier being killed.

"So they started bombing us. It was like a movie. Thousands of people running around, no real shelter anyway, people just running behind trees. We'd hear the noise, the whistle, but not know where the bomb was going to fall. Even the Cambodian freedom soldiers were running around. There was no way to fight the falling bombs. Thousands of refugees were killed along the border that day.

"The only people who didn't seem to be afraid were the American newsmen and photographers. There were some there at times during the day and that particular day, I remember seeing the photographers running around like crazy. But they were running around taking pictures! They didn't seem to care whether or not they were going to die. I couldn't believe them!

"We knew we couldn't stay in the middle of all of the fighting, we knew we had to move into Thailand, across the border. This time when we moved across, the American Red Cross helped us, made a palm tree hut for us. The

Red Cross also built a hospital there. Hundreds and hundreds of wounded people were there, screaming. The Cambodian community owes a lot to the American Red Cross."

Moving across the border into Thailand, out of Cambodia, was a step toward America, but it was only a small one. The camps were poor, dirty, and chaotic. The Cambodians felt a certain amount of protection while the volunteers and visitors from the American Red Cross and various Western European and American organizations were present during the day, but at sundown, all Westerners were forced to leave the camp.

Nightfall brought out the Thai robbers from around the countryside. There were also the Thai soldiers to fear, many of whom felt the Cambodian women and the refugees' meager property were fair game in exchange for the Cambodians squatting on the Thai border, and, always lurking in the jungle, the Khmer Rouge, who considered the refugees traitors to their country for trying to escape. The small measure of security felt in the daylight disappeared in the night. Family groups usually tried to hide or have a family member stand guard so the refugees could at least be alerted to whatever was coming for them.

"And," Paul reminds, "this was our second escape. Even during the day, it was hard to feel too much hope, too much excitement. It was difficult to keep believing that this second escape would lead us to America. It was especially difficult since our first escape had led us to the mountain."

The image of police from the Cambodian past was cruel. Frightening. Horrific. When American police were encountered, Paul and his fellow Cambodians found them to be, for the most part, courteous and respectful. But for the majority of Cambodians, the desirable path to follow was one that avoided the police altogether.

Cambodian refugees were often robbed. When Paul's family lost their television set to a thief during their first few days in America, it was not an exceptional incident. It was the rule. The new refugees, the newest ones in particular, were chosen as prey for several reasons. The first and most obvious being the fact that recently arrived Asians were easy to spot, wearing their ill-fitting hand-me-downs and clustering in ramshackle apartment buildings in the rundown East Dallas neighborhood. Any streetwise hood could assume that most of the new arrivals in America had neither the language nor the savvy to know when they were being victimized, nor could they articulate a cry for help. There was also an isolationism that worked against any group crimefighting effort. Cambodians, Laotians, and Vietnamese were all settled in the same area even though they did not share a common language nor were they natural friends. Most Americans who have not met Southeast Asians before are surprised to find out that the Khmer, the Vietnamese, the Laotian, and the Thai languages are not interchangeable. Although both Cambodia and Vietnam are primarily Buddhist countries, there are fundamental differences in the practice of the religion that separate the people spiritually. Cambodians and Vietnamese share a painful history of animosity, war, and racial prejudice. So the Little Asia neighborhood did not automatically take on any kind of cohesiveness born of loyalty. This was not an Irish, Italian, or Eastern European Jewish ghetto where everyone shared a language, a culture, and an ambition. East Dallas was not the kind of American melting pot that is so often romanticized in popular novels and television mini-series, where native sons are cheered on the playing fields or in the political arena.

Nor was Little Asia, East Dallas the neighborhood of the "miracle minority." Despite the national magazine covers that shout about the "Asian Whiz Kids" and the statistics that someone is always gathering about the number of Asian valedictorians in U.S. high schools, the children of Little Asia, some of whom had never been in any kind of classroom and many of whom didn't remember the little schooling they had had before the Khmer Rouge, were struggling through classes in a language they didn't understand, were often mocked by their American classmates for their clothes and the sounds of their language, and on several occasions were even sent out of the lunchroom hungry because their parents had failed to understand and sign the forms—printed in English—that would qualify them for the school's free hot lunch program. The children of Little Asia were expected by their parents to do well in school and were punished by them when they did not. Teachers were confounded by the fact that these refugee children with their respectful quietness, their subservience, their seeming willingness to learn often failed. They could not understand why they didn't speak up and ask for help. The American teachers could not know that a Cambodian girl or boy would not dare to question a teacher anymore than she or he would dare to defend a bad grade to parents by explaining the grading system or the class curve.

Little Asia was a neighborhood of closed doors. The locks on those doors might not work and the residents might not know how to ask the landlord to fix them . . . but they did know how to keep their eyes down and their troubles private. If someone walked in through their flimsy apartment door or climbed in through the window, tossing aside the unrepaired sash, and carted off their meager belongings, the Cambodians didn't complain. They had survived worse. They had been robbed before. They had been beaten and raped and murdered. So they wouldn't complain about that here. Not in America. It was because of their nature, their culture, but something else as well. If the Cambodians complained about America, to the police, to their school teachers, to the social workers, to the health-care volunteers, might they not be looked upon as ungrateful? And if they were judged to be ungrateful, might not America, the land of freedom and education, the land of life, send them back to Cambodia, the land of death?

Paul Thai was aware of the problems of the community. He and his family feared the rampant street crime in Little Asia. He and Marina and their small son, Chetra, along with the rest of Paul's family, suffered the heat because of broken air conditioners and struggled to keep safe with inefficient door locks—all the sorts of problems that absentee landlords in rundown neighborhoods present. But Little Asia was also home. Here, walking down Live Oak Avenue or cutting across Peak Street, you could smell good Asian food cooking. If you suffered with bad headaches, migraines, as did both Paul and his mother since Pol Pot time, you could go into an Asian store and find the proper herbs to make some medicine, or you could easily buy Tiger Balm or Monkey Holding a Peach to soothe sore muscles and backaches. In the neighborhood, you might find someone to share stories of better times in Cambodia. You could find people who looked like you, who talked like you, who understood you when you spoke, who greeted you with respect. In Little Asia, Paul's family could all be together—perhaps a little more crowded than was desirable, but still together. Paul had a good, steady, well-paying job at John A. Williams, a growing knowledge of English that, when combined with his sense of community and compassion, put him in great demand as a translator, and a beautiful wife and child. So, despite any of the disadvantages or the isolation of living in Little Asia, life was going well for the Paul Thai family.

Paul often repeats, "Cambodians are refugees, not immigrants." Although the two words are often used interchangeably, Paul emphasizes the important difference between them. "Immigrants might come to America looking for a better life. Refugees come here for a life. Period. Because they would die if they didn't come here." This is not to say that the refugee is without hope for a better life, but it does mean that "great expectations" are not necessarily a part of daily life.

In 1985, as Paul continued to discover America, an American police officer, Corporal Ronald E. Cowart, was continuing to discover Little Asia. Since the late seventies, Ron Cowart had been a positive presence in the neighborhood. Although their paths had not yet crossed, Paul (at that time, still Pov Thai) had heard of a white police officer who was becoming a major figure in Little Asia, helping the community, making a difference. And Ron Cowart would soon hear of a bright young Cambodian who might be helpful to him as a translator.

Except for the thirteen months he had spent in Vietnam on a monitor, a heavily armored and heavily armed boat that slowly made its way up and down the fingery waterways of the Mekong Delta, Ron Cowart was a lifelong Texas resident. He describes himself at age eighteen as patriotic, eagerly volunteering to serve his country in Southeast Asia. He had grown up in Fort Worth listening to his father's war stories from World War II and was anxious to have his own tales. While in Southeast Asia as a member of the Navy's Mobile Riverene Force, he remembers receiving the letters from high school friends, the ones who had gone to college, who were marching in protest and tasting the free-spirited anarchy of campus life in the sixties, telling him he was in the wrong war, doing the wrong thing. After his return, he remembers his own confusion, his own pain. He remembers reading about himself, the Vietnam Vet, described as everything from a baby killer to a drug addict to a psychotic. Cowart remembers trying to share his stories of Vietnam with his father, the World War II veteran, but being rebuffed. Vietnam wasn't a clean war, a good war. It wasn't the kind of experience you discussed in polite company. Not unless you hadn't been there and were marching to protest U.S. involvement. But if you personally had been involved, you were to speak only when spoken to. Twenty-five years later, Academy Awards and Pulitzer Prizes would be given to films and books that dealt honestly with the war, but in the late sixties and early seventies, Southeast Asia from the American soldier's point of view was not an appropriate topic of conversation.

When Cowart, age twenty-one, returned home to Texas in 1969, he entered the police academy and began college courses in the evening. He was restless about his Vietnam experience. He was restless because he was a Vietnam Vet, but he didn't fit the profile of the Vet he saw depicted in the press, on television, in books, in song lyrics. He didn't have flashbacks, use drugs, or abuse alcohol. His restlessness wasn't a part of the Vietnam Veteran syndrome every pop psychologist hashed and rehashed on talk shows. His restlessness stemmed from a job undone.

"I felt we had gone over there to do something worthwhile for the Vietnamese people, but we had let them down. We hadn't done it. We hadn't helped them. And we certainly didn't finish anything over there," Cowart says. "I felt badly about that, about the fact that so many had died, but the job remained undone."

Cowart was several years home before he found an outlet for his own unsettled feelings. A member of the Dallas Police Department's Special Operations Tactical Section, his job assignments took Cowart into only high-crime areas. On patrol in East Dallas, he remembers seeing Vietnamese children in the street. When he turned to look back at them, they were gone. Searching up and down the streets, he would see a pair of eyes peering at him from behind a curtained window. He began smelling familiar cooking smells, seeing old men squatting in doorways, hearing the syllables of a language he recalled but could not speak. His sense of déjà vu increasing, he began spending more and more time in East Dallas, asking more and more questions about the newest residents, the Asian refugees who, beginning in the seventies, were pouring into one square mile of Dallas's meanest streets.

Not everyone on the police force showed the same kind of interest. There were racial slurs and bad jokes about missing dogs showing up in the kitchens of the Asian restaurants. But Ron Cowart felt drawn to the neighborhood. Especially when he discovered the high incidence of crime in the area and the suspected higher incidence of crime that was going on unreported. He began to feel that he was being given another chance to finish a job undone.

A persuasive speaker and powerful presence, Cowart convinced both corporations and individuals to donate goods, money, and time to help the people of the Little Asia community. Cowart's wife, whom he had married in 1977, was a teacher of English as a Second Language at Spence Middle School and was already involved in the community because of her commitment to her Asian pupils. Dr. Melinda Cowart drew her husband further into Little Asia with her growing knowledge of the family problems and cultural differences faced by her young students.

Because Cowart learned to understand the character of the Little Asia community, their shyness with Americans, their fear of authority, their reluctance to report crime, or to even complain about poor treatment or substandard living conditions, he knew he would have to come up with new methods to reach the Asian residents, to fight the rising crime statistics in the area. Facing age-old prejudices and fears without even a common language didn't discourage Cowart. He seemed to welcome the challenge.

One of his earliest solutions? If a uniformed American is an object of fear for the Cambodians, one should simply demystify the uniform. With the sponsorship of his own church, Highland Baptist, Cowart founded a Boy Scout Explorer Post in the neighborhood, making sure each boy wore his uniform and earned his merit badges by actively engaging in crime prevention activities. One of the first major activities of Troop 68 was to send the thirty Asian scouts out into the neighborhood with the tools to install peepholes in every apartment front door. The Asian Scouts felt worthwhile and important and the community was served. And served by people in uniform—Ron in his police uniform and their own sons and daughters in their Scout uniforms.

This was a start. But Cowart, as well as the core of other committed volunteers in the Dallas Little Asia community—Charles Kemp and the people who worked with him in community health care, Chuck Morris and the other clergymen who went door-to-door on home visits, and the scores of caseworkers who took on the overwhelming task of settling the new families, finding homes, food, clothing, and stretching their meager budgets to cover all the expenses the refugees would encounter starting over in America—knew that a peephole in the door would keep away neither the wolf of hunger nor the human beasts of prey who saw Little Asia as ripe for plunder.

Ron Cowart, soft-spoken, but with a rapid delivery and an unstoppable recitation of facts and figures peppering his monologue, will tell anyone and everyone how he saw the problem in Little Asia.

"We had to earn the trust of these people. That takes time. And a lot of police officers didn't have the time or patience. We needed to have a presence in the community, a constant presence. The Asian people were not going to come to us and report crime or complain or give us information until they trusted us and saw that we were there to be their friends, their advocates."

The idea of a police storefront located in the Little Asia neighborhood might not seem revolutionary. It would certainly make sense to station officers where they could do the most good, and a high-crime area like Little Asia was as likely a location as any. Not only were there a large number of robberies and assaults, but drug traffickers were known to operate in the neighborhood. It was believed that gang activity in the area was accelerating. Stationing some of Dallas's finest in the heart of Little Asia would make for good policing and for good public relations. Newspaper and magazine articles were beginning to feature the problems faced by the refugees and public sympathy was growing.

Because Cowart had started the Explorer Post and was so active in volunteer activities in the Little Asia community, Deputy Police Chief Lowell Canaday asked Cowart to act as a liaison between the community and the department. After walking through the neighborhood, meeting the people, talking to the shopkeepers, listening to the old and the young talk about their new country and their old country, Corporal Cowart went back to his Chief and recommended setting up the East Dallas Storefront. It would be a community police operation located in the heart of Little Asia. It would be staffed by police officers and police service officers—uniformed members of the department who assist the regular officers. They would extend a welcoming hand to the community, help with social service needs including translating, and familiarize the new Asian Texans with American customs and crime-fighting information. It would work to eradicate the old fears and prejudices against law enforcement officers that the Asians, particularly the Cambodians, carried with them from their homeland. The storefront made crime-fighting sense and it made public relations sense. One might think that Ron Cowart, with his fresh and innovative proposal, would be the man of the hour in the eyes of the department.

Corporals, however, are rarely the men of the hour. Cowart explains that a storefront is a concept that usually comes from the top and filters down through the ranks. Rarely, in an organization such as the Dallas Police Department, does a grass-roots idea, planted by a lowly corporal, sprout up through the chain of command, then bloom. The East Dallas Storefront is an idea that, by all rights, *should* have withered on the vine.

"When I proposed the storefront to Chief, at that time Billy Prince, he thought it was a good idea, but threw it back at me. Where would the money come from, the staff, and so forth. So I did the paperwork. I wrote up all the forms and hand-carried every one of them to the appropriate offices. I was doing a lot of talking. You know, saying stuff like he agrees if you agree, so if you'll sign this authorization, then he'll sign, then going back to personnel or wherever and saying look at who signed this. I'm authorized now to do this, just sign here and I'll take it up to so-and-so's office. It was a hectic time.

"The big question was the money. Always is. So I decided that if I got the money from another source to start the storefront, and the place was a success, the department would have to keep it going. So I set up a meeting with some people at the Meadows Foundation here in Dallas. They told me it took a certain amount of time for a grant proposal to be considered and approved, and I just asked them if they could do it right away."

This is Cowart's style. Simple. Direct. Relentless. Knowing both in his head and his heart that he could be a problem solver not a paper shuffler, believing that he and the storefront could actually make a difference in East Dallas, he simply did not take "no" for an answer. He did not even take "maybe" for an answer.

By circumventing channels, by standing in front of people at their desks and waiting for them to say yes, by sheer perseverence and presence, Cowart got the grant which he took to the Dallas Police Department. Since lack of funds had been the only reason to reject Cowart's proposal for the East Dallas Storefront and Cowart had eliminated that consideration, the department gave Cowart the okay.

In some ways, it was a qualified okay. Corporal Ron Cowart had come up with the idea of the storefront so Corporal Ron Cowart had to come up with the reality of the storefront. It would be up to him to find the building, interview and hire suitable staff, publicize it, and make it run.

It was understood by the department and by Cowart that storefronts make for good publicity, good community relations. Everyone knew or could imagine the photo opportunities and television news features that would showcase the Dallas Police Department when the storefront opened its doors. But because of Cowart and his vision, this storefront held more promise. Cowart maintained that this police presence, this reaching out to the Asian community would reduce crime and would be a valuable introduction to America and American values for the Asian newcomers.

But Cowart did not want to patronize. Cowart did not want to Americanize. Cowart wanted to set up an exchange of cultural information. He had walked the streets of the neighborhood and had earned the respect of the people. He had done this not by imposing his American presence on the Asian residents, but by learning to greet them with respect, palms pressed together, saying *chumriap sua,* by learning to address the elders rather than the children, by asking the kinds of direct, yet polite, questions that would lead to a true revelation of the community's needs. Cowart did not take on this project only to teach. He accepted the challenge because he was eager to learn.

That is what made him, in the eyes of Paul Thai, a "hero to the Asian people."

But before Cowart could take on any of these heroic proportions for Paul or any others in the Cambodian community, he had to make the storefront work. He found the location—a former machine shop at 1327 North Peak Street. In spite of the big front windows that faced the street, the place was dark and dirty. The Meadows Foundation grant, pooled with funds from the department, gave Cowart one hundred sixty thousand dollars for renovation, utilities and the salaries of three police service officers, better known as PSOs.

"The thing that hung a lot of people up with my idea in the first place was that I insisted that the storefront be staffed with Asian Police Service Officers," says Cowart. "We had to have Asians in uniform. I saw that it was an absolute necessity to have translators—but not just people who spoke English as well as Laotian or Vietnamese or Khmer, but people who understood cultural differences. The department thought I was crazy—you know everybody asking if I really thought I was going to put these Asians in uniform and teach them to be police officers and all that. But I knew that it was the only way to make this work, the only way to make the Asians living in the neighborhood trust us."

Since roughly thirty-three thousand Southeast Asians lived in the Dallas area, and approximately four thousand Cambodians and several hundred Vietnamese and Laotians lived in Little Asia, one might think that finding one Vietnamese, one Laotian, and one Cambodian officer for the new East Dallas Community Police and Refugee Affairs Center might be a relatively simple project.* But as Ron Cowart remembers it, the process was far from simple.

"Once I was authorized to search for the people to fill the PSO slots, I had to have a way to publicize the job openings. There was a radio station, KNON, that had programs presented for and by various ethnic groups. On Saturday mornings, they had a Cambodian show which was mostly politi-

---

*Although the storefront was established in 1985, these population figures are taken from the public files of 1986 since statistics are generally gathered and compiled from the previous year. Because of the difficulty in keeping an accurate area census, they are approximate.

cal—you know, what's going on in Cambodia, Vietnam, etc., and they played some music. Then they gave me ten minutes or so to talk about crime prevention. So during my ten minutes, I presented our needs. I said we needed someone to work within the Dallas Police Department, to wear the uniform, and work in crime prevention, criminal investigation, and community relations. Then I wrote up the job description and took it to the Cambodian newspaper, the *Voice of Khmer*. I wrote a corner column with crime prevention tips—which I just took from the police community relations department—and I put the word out there. I also spread the word by mentioning it through one of the translators who assisted me when I walked through the community, visiting door-to-door.

"Then they started appearing. I was allowed to use the Dallas/Fort Worth Refugee Agency for interviews. I saw applicants one at a time and would go over translated forms with them or give them complex crime prevention information and give them ten minutes to translate that into Khmer, then I would have to go to someone else, someone who was fluent in English and Khmer, and have them check the grammar. I would also give oral tests. I would read from some crime prevention report and these poor guys would have to watch my eyes and lips to translate as I was speaking, while others in the office wandered in and out, staring at us, wondering why two people were talking at the same time. And there was usually a third guy who listened to make sure the applicant's translation and grammar were correct. It was quite a circus.

"A lot of the applicants were really good at translating because they had worked with U.S. government agencies overseas. They could write perfectly, but unfortunately, they couldn't keep up in oral translation. Or their English was unintelligible because of heavy French accents. Day in and day out, I listened and interviewed. I would interview Cambodians for two-and-one-half hours, then rest for thirty minutes. Then I would interview Vietnamese, then take a rest. Then Laotian. By 5 P.M. I was really tired. I sat there all day, drinking coffee and listening. I never really lost patience, but the frustration level was very high. I went home at 5 P.M. and started speaking in broken English to my wife, Melinda. I'd say, 'I go store now,' or 'I go to eat now.' It was like the officers who work in West Dallas which is primarily black. They start talking black street talk. It really isn't meant to be patronizing, it's just impossible not to pick it up."

The people who poured into the refugee office to be interviewed were an interesting group. And Coward found his own sympathies running high. "I felt incredibly sorry for people who wanted so badly to work with us. Especially the Vietnamese. I would just talk to them for fifteen minutes or so, to put them at their ease, and they would tell me how they worked for the government in their own country, as engineers or in intelligence. They missed that, they were very patriotic people and wanted to work for the government in their new country. The reason they weren't passing with me was their heavy French accents. I could barely understand their English. So I would put them in a reserve column. I had a very large reserve column, but as far as likely candidates for the PSO positions, things were not working out."

At the same time Cowart was interviewing, he was trying to get the building open. He would do the paperwork connected with the funding, conduct some interviews, then check with Civil Service to see if any of the applicants who had made it that far were passing the necessary civil service exam. "I learned that the money was coming through for the storefront, but I wasn't sure I was going to have anyone to work there. The police department was so bureaucratic, the chain of command was so long. And because some people saw this as a social service operation rather than as police work, not everyone was as eager as I was to make it work. Since this was coming from the bottom up, from a lowly corporal off the street, I had to be the advocate in every respect, every phase of the operation. A friend of mine was the city councilman from this district, so everything that had to go through the council, I ran by him first. For instance, the budget proposal—he sensitized them to the issues. Then I lobbied council members elsewhere. They all liked the idea and were glad that I came to them with it. Everything was coming together. Except that I had no officers."

Cowart had kept a running list of applicants. Since there was not a list of likely candidates—those who could translate as well as speak fluent, understandable English—he went to his marginal list, his reserve list. Deciding that he would probably have to staff the office with officers who either had translation skills, grammatical skills, or spoke effective English, since he had found no one yet who combined all three, he began asking some of the applicants to take the various exams that would be required for the job.

"Some took the civil service exam and passed," Cowart remembers, "and some didn't." Those that passed the civil service test went on to take the polygraph test. Most didn't pass that. The few who made it through those two went on to the psychological testing. Then they bombed out there."

Cowart could be a friend and an advocate for the Asian people in almost every respect. During the interviewing process he took as much time as everyone needed and tried to relax the applicants, to help them through any anxiety that would interfere with their performance in oral translation. But his influence stopped there. "I couldn't be their advocate on the civil service, the polygraph, or the psychological testing. They were on their own there. I couldn't change anything or interfere with those tests.

"But I found out that those tests are extremely biased. The department will admit it, but it hasn't been changed because it's never been challenged in court. It's extremely difficult for Asians, for anyone who is of the Asian culture, to successfully get through the psychological exam.

"For instance, you can't be a homosexual and join the Dallas Police Department. But that isn't what they ask—they don't ask, 'Are you a homosexual?' But they do ask if you've ever held hands with a member of your own sex. Or if you ever put your arm around someone of your own sex. Or if you've ever kissed someone and so on. And with Oriental cultures as well as some European cultures, men hold hands with each other when they walk. They put their arms around each other. In the river, they've taken baths together. When I was in Vietnam—well, we were a bunch of rowdy rednecks in those days—and I can remember one of the reasons we questioned why we were there. We thought the whole country was gay! No wonder they're all going to hell here—they're all holding hands with each other!"

There were also questions on the psychological exam concerning spirits and belief in the supernatural. These doomed many Asians to failure. Cowart remembers listening to many stories of spirits during his door-to-door visits in the neighborhoods. "People would explain to me why they kept so many candles in their apartment, to light the way for the spirits," says Cowart.

Buddhists believe in honoring the spirits of their dead ancestors and they believe that those spirits are with them. They believe in reincarnation. According to Paul, many Cambodians believe that there are thirty-two spirits that control the head, the mind. These thirty-two spirits must be kept in harmony. Touching the head, or tousling the hair of a Cambodian adult or child, is a grave error. Nothing should pass between the head and the spirits that surround it. Paul gestures to his own head when he talks about his: "It doesn't really matter for me anymore! My spirits are already very messed up."

In addition to the department's psychological tests which were responsible for Cowart's dwindling reserve list of applicants, there were also officers in the department who consistently told Cowart that the storefront project would fail. "They'd say to me, these people don't respect law and order. These people don't trust police. These people don't trust authority. Well, in a way, they were right about the lack of trust. That was my whole point about starting the storefront.

"The Asians didn't have trust because where they came from, uniformed authority was so corrupt. But as for respecting law and order . . . these are people who are extremely patriotic and loyal to their leaders. When I held meetings in the community, 150 people would show up. There was no food served or music played. They just came to listen to me. I felt like Billy Graham! That's how I learned to be confident when I spoke around here. Everywhere I went, after people knew me and began to trust me, people opened their doors and came out, following me. A simple walk in the neighborhood would become an hour-and-a-half long because everybody came out to listen. These people have plenty of respect."

Just when Ron was beginning to wear down from the interviewing process, he found two members of his team in rapid succession. Leck Keovilay, a Buddhist monk, had come to the United States as a student and was caught here when Laos fell. He worked with Asian refugees in New York and Los Angeles before coming to the Dallas area to take a job as a caseworker. As a tireless community volunteer, Leck had been a willing and apt translator when called upon by the Dallas Police Department. When he decided to apply for the storefront position, Cowart grew cautiously optimistic.

When Thao Dam, a fifty-two-year-old Vietnamese refugee, came to talk to Ron, Cowart began breathing even more easily. Dam, well-known in the Asian community, had also helped the police department before when they needed a translator. A former civil affairs officer for the Nationalist army, Thao Dam's job had been to guide South Vietnamese villagers away from encroaching battle lines. He had been resettling displaced civilians, finding them shelter, food, and medical care for fifteen years when Saigon fell in 1975. In joining Cowart's operation at the storefront, he could continue doing the same work here in America.

With Thao Dam and Leck Keovilay on the team, Ron Cowart had two-thirds of his novel storefront squad, but he had 4,000 Cambodians in the Little Asia neighborhood who needed a Cambodian officer they could trust.

Cowart had heard the Kipling quotation "East is East and West is West and never the twain shall meet," but discovered its veracity for himself. "It's true that with the East and West, everything is the opposite. Take charity for instance. Westerners are guilt oriented. We want to work off our guilt by doing good, doing something charitable. With Asians, everything is directed toward internal suffering. That's how they work out their guilt or their grief or whatever. If you go out in public and and grieve or expect sympathy or praise, you're not suffering enough. It's how well you deal with adversity in this life that determines your status in the next life. So the Asians need to suffer. They won't complain about housing problems. They strove to get to America and they need to work their way up, to suffer along the way.

"It's defeating for me to come in and pretend to be a savior and say I can get rid of the housing problems, because I know it's good for them to suffer—which of course I can't say because it sounds like I want them to suffer. I can say something like this—that I love being in America and in America we don't want to see people suffer and it goes against my grain to see suffering or to allow conditions of suffering, and I want to do something about it because I do have solutions.

"I needed officers with me that could help me get this across without making me look like The Ugly American," says Ron. "Thao Dam could do that. Leck Keovilay could do that, but I still had not found a likely Cambodian candidate."

What could Cowart do, under pressure from the department, from the city council, from the various social service organizations, corporations, and individuals whom he had lobbied in an effort to make the storefront a reality?

"I prayed," says Cowart simply, "and lo and behold, the next day, a preacher himself brings in Pov Thai." Cowart laughs, "It'd made a good story for *Guidepost* magazine, wouldn't it?"

Hearing about the storefront position and hearing, too, that no one had been found to fill it, Chuck Morris persuaded his number-one translator to come in and apply for the police service officer position. Chuck knew that Paul Thai, then Pov Thai, had all the right stuff. Pov Thai was bilingual, culturally aware, unafraid and community spirited. He had arrived in Dallas at a young enough age to be a willing student of English and American customs, yet he was old enough to remember Cambodia, to remember his family and his homeland's traditions. He revered and respected his elders, but was ready to embrace the mores of his new home. Chuck knew the kind of man Ron Cowart needed and knew that Pov would be perfect.

Cowart remembers seeing Pov Thai for the first time. "He came in wearing a serious expression and a suit several sizes too large for him, and looking so young!" Pov Thai's youthful looks were a problem. Asians revere age. Pov Thai, looking even younger than his twenty-two years, might not represent the kind of authority figure that Cowart needed to staff the storefront. Leck, at forty-two, was a young man, but was taller and had a larger frame. His face was more weathered, and despite his almost constant smile, he gave an older appearance. Thao Dam, at age fifty-two, presented the perfect face for his job in the community—older, wiser, with eyes that had clearly seen too much suffering.

Cowart, however, was desperate and no longer had the luxury of passing any judgments based on appearance. He began interviewing Pov Thai and immediately knew he had found his man. Cowart found the same quality in Pov Thai that Chuck Morris had found—the ability to understand and translate fine concepts of thought in addition to simply exchanging the words of one language for another. The combination of intelligence, motivation, and compassion that had made Paul invaluable as an assistant at The New Life Cambodian Baptist Church was the mix of qualities that Cowart had been looking for.

"I knew that Asians revered age, of course, and that younger people or younger-looking people often wrinkled up their faces and squinted their eyes when they had their photographs taken so they would look older," Ron Cowart says, "but Pov Thai was the right man." Boyish face or no, Cowart wanted Pov as a PSO.

Ron Cowart and Chuck Morris had agreed that Pov Thai would make the ideal police service officer for the new East Dallas Storefront, but Pov Thai remembers wrestling with a different set of feelings at the time.

"I had heard about Ron Cowart before I met him that day. I knew he was doing many good things in the community. I was happy to go, meet with him, and talk to him about his job. But," Paul shakes his head remembering, "there were many problems with me taking the job."

First, Paul was uncertain about whether he could pass the tests he would have to take for the job. He had heard that the civil service exam might be difficult—so many Asians, because of their meticulous test-taking method, were unable to complete enough questions to pass. Although he could be confident of his own sound mind, the police department psychological test could be an insurmountable hurdle for Paul. He already knew of the many cultural differences that might make him seem mentally "unsound" if he gave Cambodian answers to American questions. Paul was scrupulously honest, but the polygraph test was an unknown and potentially frightening procedure. Thao Dam, reminded of the severe physical torture he had endured in a Vietnamese concentration camp after Saigon fell in 1975, had become hysterical when the electrodes were first attached to his chest.

Those three tests were obstacles, but Ron Cowart assured Paul that he could easily surmount them. Paul, however, had other major concerns.

Americans, familiar with the term "identity crisis," could empathize with one of Paul's dilemmas. "I loved being in America and I knew that working with the police, working with Ron Cowart would be a way to help my own people in the community, to help them be at home in America. But I was worried about putting on the uniform. I talked to an older Cambodian man and told him that I would be able to help everyone, help them give their complaints and get them better-equipped apartments, improve their living conditions. And this old man said to me that this was not right. That if a man is starving to death and you offer him a hamburger and he says, no, I don't want your hamburger, I want steak, the one who reaches out the helping hand is going to take it away. No steak and not even any hamburger and the hungry man will starve. The old man was describing the Cambodians who might complain about their living conditions in America. He thought we would seem ungrateful if we complained and asked for more. If we asked for steak instead of taking the hamburger that was offered, maybe we would be sent back to Cambodia. This made me think about the nature of the job I would be doing."

Paul, trying to view the position that was being offered from every angle, considered Ron Cowart. "At first, when Chuck Morris told me about Ron, I thought, *hmmm,* an anglo man trying to do something for our people? Then Ron talked to me and told me about the storefront program, the plan for it. He talked about the killing fields and what my people went through. He talked about the mass graves. He really knew about everything. Then he talked about the criminal elements here that prey on the Cambodians because so many are still afraid of the police. So I knew that this guy, Ron Cowart, has the same heart as I do. I had heard of Ron Cowart, the man who people said was in the Asian community twenty-four hours a day, and now I knew that what people said about him was true . . . that he really cared about us."

Paul still hesitated. Politely, he told Ron that he would think it over.

On the one side, Paul had heard from the man who believed starving people should not make demands, should accept the hamburger and not ask for steak, but Paul began hearing from the other side. Asian leaders in the community approached Paul's father and persuaded him that his son should take the job. With the community elders and his father lobbying him to say yes, Paul grew closer to making a commitment.

There was just one wrinkle left to iron out.

Paul was, at the time, making $8.50 per hour working as a supervisor for the John A. Williams company. The position of Dallas Police Department Police Service Officer would pay approximately seven dollars per hour. Paul Thai, an American resident for only four years, was being asked by those whom he respected to do something virtually un-American—to voluntarily take a pay cut. From the time of Paul's arrival in Dallas he had been taught that in America it is vital to get a job, to make money for the rent, for the bills that will accumulate monthly. Paul's dream of going to school was delayed so he could take a job. He gave up any leisure time that he might have enjoyed to study and volunteer as a translator so he could improve his English skills which would, in turn, lead him to better and more high-paying jobs. Paul had been told by caseworkers and been taught by television and radio programs that getting ahead meant working hard and working hard would hold rewards. Now he was being offered a position that would mean longer hours, higher risk, and less money.

Marina, Paul's wife, was understandably upset. The family was still living with Paul's father and mother, brothers and sister. His oldest brother, Mao, had also moved back in . . . with his three children. The family had moved to a small rental house, but with the increase in family members, there was still a dramatic shortage of space and privacy. A reduction in salary would do little to solve the family's daily, weekly, and monthly financial problems.

The risk factor was also something that worried Marina. She might not have been as familiar with American culture as Paul, but she did understand the meaning of the word *police* and knew that putting on a uniform could be dangerous for Paul. His mother, too, cautioned Paul not to take the job. She had already seen her son take too many chances in his young life.

Paul considered all the voices. The community leaders encouraged him to take the job, and his father told him to take the job. Marina and his mother shook their heads. Paul listened to Ron Cowart, a white man who was devoting all his waking hours to improving conditions in Little Asia. Paul smiles when he remembers Ron's talks with him. "Ronny talked and talked about my people. About what happened in Cambodia, about what was happening here. He was a good talker, Ronny was!"

Paul also listened to his own inner voice. "I thought more and more about everything. I had been working as a printer for about three-and-a-half years. But I knew they needed me in the community. And working for the police department would be a career, not just a job. And I thought it would help me with my education, too.

"So I took the tests . . . the Civil Service and Ronny told me I passed. I took the psychological test and Ronny told me I passed. I took the polygraph and Ronny told me I passed. I thought more and more about it and decided that I couldn't think about money only. I had to take the job. I told Ron that I would take it and he said real quickly, 'Good, you start July 10,' and that was that."

5

Cops

In Cambodia, my master always told me, and this is the Buddhist belief—you do good to get good. I heard a pastor say, though, that the Christian way is not to do good to get good, but to have faith in God to get rewards. Even though I am a Christian now—no belief in reincarnation—I still believe in doing good.

—Paul Thai

When Paul made the decision to join Corporal Ron Cowart at the East Dallas Storefront, the building on Peak Street was still a dingy, empty space. "No desks, no chairs, no equipment," remembers Paul. Of course, the official opening was not to be until December of 1985, so there was time to furnish the office. There was also time for Paul and his coworkers, Leck Keovilay and Thao Dam, to get acquainted.

Police service officers, unlike those aspiring to be regular police officers, do not normally attend the entire course of study at the police academy. There is an abbreviated program of two to three weeks that serves as job training. Corporal Ron Cowart, as part of his master plan for the East Dallas Storefront, insisted that his PSOs follow the full seventeen-week police academy course, except for the firearms training. The PSOs would carry nightsticks, but not guns. He felt that the academy training was essential.

Pov (Paul), Leck, and Thao would all be working in a high-crime area and would be wearing the uniform of the Dallas Police Department. It was important that they understood the honor and responsibility that went along with the uniform. Cowart wanted them in good physical and mental shape, to serve their community and to serve as backup for the crime fighting he knew they would have to do there. That reasoning alone would justify their attendance at the academy, but there was another aspect to it that Cowart felt was going to be key in the storefront's success.

Cowart had spent time getting to know the community, getting to know the individuals that made up Little Asia. As he immersed himself deeper in the customs and beliefs of the different Asian groups, his understanding and respect for the people deepened as well. He talked to his wife, Melinda, about the families she met through her work at school, he talked to the social service workers in the neighborhood, he read what he was able to find, but most of all he listened to the people. He had known one face of Southeast Asia from the time he served in Vietnam, but in getting to know his new Asian neighbors in Dallas, he began to see many different layers of personality.

Cowart began to understand "face" in the Asian sense of the word. He knew that the police academy training would give the PSOs honor and status in their own communities. In an area where one not only had to fight crime, but also had to overcome the people's fear and lack of trust for authority, it was important to show them that their own representative, their own PSO was a trained, competent, trusted member of the Dallas Police Department. In giving Pov, Lek, and Thao the entire course of training, the Dallas Police Department was both challenging them and honoring them. When they completed the course, their own pride would be a positive factor in the execution of their duties.

At the same time Ron Cowart was learning about "face" and learning to respect the concept, Paul was learning about the American penchant for finding humor in another person's pain—and learning about the American custom of laughing at oneself, and learning not to take one's self so seriously.

Paul was and is proud of his police training, but remembers the first few days of the physical training with a shudder. "We three had never done anything like jumping jacks before. So when we did it, we must have looked pretty funny. I felt like I was flying," Paul shakes his head, "and Thao Dam, he was so old to be starting an exercise program like this, he was fifty-two, and so skinny, we were all worried about him. The captain who was leading us started laughing so hard. He stopped everybody and told them to watch the three guys in the back do it. So everybody turned around and watched us. God! We did about fifty jumping jacks and I felt my migraine headache coming, I was getting so dizzy, and I said, 'Oh no, I'm gone,' and I passed out!

"The captain said, 'No more passing out,' and I didn't pass out again. The second or third time after that, I began to enjoy the exercise. It began to feel good. But the first time . . ." Paul shakes his head ruefully.

Another positive aspect of the police academy training was the development of bonds between the three men—Paul, Leck, and Thao. Ron Cowart knew the feelings of camaraderie that develop through shared experiences— the armed services, the police force—and he knew that these three men would have to learn to overcome cultural differences of their own in order to work together. Paul remembers the first days: "I thought, *hmmm,* I'm going to be working with a Vietnamese man? Thao Dam? Then we actually started working together. I started getting to know Thao Dam." Paul smiles and says, "Thao Dam is like my brother now. Leck, too. We are all like brothers now."

One of the first things Ron Coward did was put in what they called the Asian hotline, to provide translation services for anyone who might need them to report a crime. They offered translators who could handle Khmer, Vietnamese, Laotian, Korean, Mandarin, and Cantonese. Several times they got calls asking for someone who could speak "Oriental." Cowart remembers, "I was used to general stereotyping that way, so I would just casually ask what kind of Oriental. Once, a police officer from the Irving department answered, 'Oh, male or female, it doesn't matter.'

"Unfortunately," Ron Cowart says, "that's a true story and not an isolated or unusual one."

The "speaking Oriental" is an anecdote that Cowart often uses in his speeches and presentations to civic groups. Audience members, for the most part, shake their heads, but they probably shouldn't be too surprised at the confusion about Asians, about the different nationalities, languages, histories, cultures. For most American-born Americans, knowledge of the East, of Asia, of the Orient is rather nonspecific. The stereotypes most prevalent are that the Japanese are leaders in technology, the Chinese built the U.S. railroads, were relegated to laundries, and now provide marvelous carryout food, and the Koreans raise the children who get the highest scores on standardized tests.

Although the Vietnam War raised the collective consciousness of many Americans about Southeast Asia, it was, for the most part, an emotional response. Some young Americans, like Ron Cowart, enlisted in the armed services to fight Communism, to claim their war, and to become heroes. They knew little about the country in which they fought, knew less about the people they were defending, and returned home unheralded, confused, and angry.

Many of the young Americans who stayed on college campuses vigorously protested American involvement in Southeast Asia. They engaged in sit-ins, teach-ins, and witnessed street theater demonstrations that graphically portrayed the immorality of war. However, for most of the students who marched, who listened, who sat-in, the war was the focal point. The American involvement was the immoral issue. Americans were shocked in 1990 when a test revealed that a majority of high school students could not locate Vietnam on a map, yet several of the most vigorous war protesters of the sixties would have been at a loss to explain the history and significance of the war in Southeast Asia. Few average Americans could delineate the cultural differences between the Laotians, the Thais, the Cambodians and the Vietnamese . . . or felt they needed to.

Until the Southeast Asians ended up on the wrong side of those Chinese-built railroad tracks in several American cities, the average American didn't really need to know that the average Cambodian and the average Vietnamese would be, at best, volatile neighbors. The unschooled but good-hearted church volunteer who goes in to help a Cambodian family adjust to life in America and introduces them to their nice Vietnamese neighbors next door—assuming they'd have lots of things in common—might be surprised at the tension and hostility he or she encounters. Racial prejudice, fear, and hatred based on skin color is not the unique property of the Westerner. There are Asians, too, who discriminate against others because of the darkness or lightness of another's skin. There are the light-skinned Cambodians who whisper to each other that the darker-skinned Vietnamese are dog-eaters and there are Vietnamese who laugh at the gullibility of the backward Cambodian peasant. There are those Cambodians who rejoice that the Vietnamese liberated them from the Khmer Rouge in 1979 and there are those Cambodians who seethe with emotion over the continued Vietnamese involvement in their homeland.

The mixed emotions and memories of the late sixties and early seventies continue to be dissected, romanticized, debunked, and, most probably, over-worked. Realistic portrayals of the Vietnam War and the war at home in the U.S. have been given successful form in the eighties and nineties with films such as *Platoon* and *Born on the Fourth of July.* The cost of theatrical production has reached new heights with the budget for *Miss Saigon,* which opened on Broadway in April 1991. In addition to the financial headlines inspired by *Miss Saigon,* this same play generated a controversy over its casting of a white actor in the lead role—the same white actor, Jonathan Pryce, who had played the part in London. Led by the few prominent Asian members of the theatrical unions who pointed out the few available roles for Asians and the unfairness of casting a white actor in a role that could give an enormous opportunity to an Asian actor, a protest was staged. Accusations flew, editorials were written, the play was cancelled, then, after a brief cooling-off period, the play was rescheduled. The producer agreed to actively seek Asian actors for the lesser roles by advertising in the many Asian newspapers that exist in major cities and has banned the use of yellow face paint and devices for approximating "Asian" eyes. Although the protesters might celebrate a victory here—fair casting and a recognition of the availability of Asian talent—the irony, of course, is that few Asians outside the theatrical world will ever hear of the play, the controversy, or the victory. The price of a theater ticket on Broadway guarantees that. Even if, after a successful run, *Miss Saigon* is taped for a television showing which would make it available to a wider audience, it will be long after the protest and victory are considered newsworthy.

Literature, too, has mined Vietnam for material, resulting in best-sellers by Phillip Caputo and Tim O'Brien as well as serious critical studies and college courses with titles such as "The Literature of Vietnam." In this world of popular culture, both the sixties student protester and the American soldier can find identifiable characters while the next generation, their children, discovery the history behind the peace-sign earrings and tie-dyed clothes once again fashionable after twenty years.

But for the newest Americans, the Asian refugees so dependent on popular culture for their information about America, there are few recognizable icons. The only television show in recent history that actually featured the story of an Asian was "Kung Fu" which starred American actor David Carradine (no ban on yellow makeup or false Asian eyes was in effect during the filming of this show) as a peaceful martial arts expert who was forced into confrontation after confrontation as he wandered through the Old West. The mixed messages of that show support the confusion and stereotyping that abounds.

Paul Thai, who on a walk through the Little Asia neighborhood in 1989 flinches and shakes his head when a young black man sitting on the steps of a run-down apartment building, yells out, "Hey, hi Japanese!" says he seldom has time to watch any television. His children love cartoons, and his wife Marina names "General Hospital" as one of her favorite shows, but Paul has never seen Johnny Carson or "LA Law." He does smile as he thinks of one program. "There is one show that comes on around ten o'clock every night that I really love to watch if I'm home. It makes me laugh and seems very true and very funny. So if I'm not studying for exams or writing papers, I watch

'Sanford and Son.' " And although many might agree that the star of "Sanford and Son," Redd Foxx, is a funny comedian, few black Americans would want his portrayal of a cantankerous junk man to be taken as a representative role model. When "Kung Fu" meets Fred Sanford, confusion about who is really who is likely to occur.

For an American who aspires to be a law enforcement officer, there are scores of fictional role models. These models range from the fantastic and the mythic to the glamorous, the comic, and the grittily realistic. Preschool boys and girls understand the concepts of right and wrong, heroes and villains, and from the cartoon shows directed at them, imagine themselves as "Masters of the Universe," "Superman," "Wonderwoman," "Spiderman," and "She-ra." Young children of the eighties cherish their ghostbuster de-slimers and Batman pajamas in the same manner that their parents hid their Dick Tracy and Captain Midnight decoder rings under their pillows. These superheroes and super cops, no matter what their power source, share common goals. They put the bad guys away. They make the world safer. And whenever possible, they cooperate with local law enforcement agencies.

There are the glamorous cops of daytime television. Every soap opera has its local cop or detective, its Frisco Jones or Robert Scorpio or Anna Lavery, who, despite his or her small-town beat, manages to solve crimes of earth-shattering proportions, all the while carrying on romantic involvements and sharing the numerous subplots of a "General Hospital."

The comic cops are perennial popular character types as evidenced by the popularity of the movie *Police Academy* and its infinite number of sequels. Television shows, too, have built laugh tracks around the antics of bumbling, inefficient cops with hearts of gold. From the classic "Car 54, Where Are You?" to "Barney Miller," the situation comedy genre has mined the humor found in men and women who wear badges for a living.

The dramatic television show, such as "Hill Street Blues" that attempts to be realistic, to show how it really is to be a cop, to fight crime on urban streets, has been wildly successful. The ensemble cast of actors who played the characters from the Hill Street station took on an eerie reality for viewers, some who found themselves undeniably shaken when a fictional cop would die in the line of duty.

These fictional cops, these role models, whether funny or serious, realistic or fantastic, share another trait besides that of good intentions. They are American. Black and white. Even the lone Asian that comes to mind—the character played by Jack Soo on "Barney Miller"—was American. These cops are the epitome of the Western hero—brave, honest, and romantic.

The Dallas Police Department's Asian PSOs were also the epitome of the Western hero . . . and more. They were brave in acting against their own apprehensions about what and who police were in their native countries; they were honest, scrupulous and meticulous both by nature and out of respect for their new country; and they were romantic in the sense that they were pioneers, emerging role models for their community members. Their dissimilarity to the Western hero was, of course, that they weren't Western— unless one counts the fact that they lived in Texas.

Because Pov, Leck, and Thao were quite obviously Asian, they received a great deal of attention, both at the police academy and in the newspapers. Some of the attention they received, such as being singled out during their first jumping jacks, was less than desirable. But the other attention, the newspaper stories, the television news features, the publicity that surrounded their recruitment and the opening of the East Dallas Storefront was essential.

Ron Cowart understood the power of this press. The Dallas Police Department would continue to smile upon the operation as long as the operation continued to improve public relations. Cowart's ability to marshall volunteers was considerable, and his talent for getting the right people in the right places at the right time—when the cameras were clicking and rolling—has become legendary. As he unloaded bags of rice in front of the storefront, one of the police officers assigned to the Peak Street Station grumbled to a Dallas newspaper reporter that Ron always scheduled rice deliveries on a day when a photographer was visiting.

Ron was used to hearing grumbling from other police officers. The storefront kept nearly a ton of rice, packaged in five-pound bags stored in a backroom closet. A rack of donated clothes stood in the back room, with large plastic garbage bags of more clothes tucked under it. Although the staff has maintained from the beginning that there was not enough room to store clothing, some giveaways remain because there are those in the neighborhood who will not go to the church basements or social service agencies. They will only come to the storefront. No matter what they need, the storefront is the answer. For the regular police officers who have served there, much of the storefront duty has smacked of social work rather than police work. And that is what much of the grumbling is about.

Cowart strongly maintains that he is not a social worker, but a cop. In order to do police work in Little Asia, however, community relations must first be established, then nurtured, until the newest Asian residents are comfortable enough to raise their eyes to a police officer. When that happens, crimes will be reported. Crimes will be solved. From the beginning, Paul, Leck, and Thao, the Asian Police Service Officers, were to be the links that hold this fragile system together.

Paul was never told his grade on the final exam at the police academy that first time through for PSO training. "They just told me I passed. And told Leck and Thao that they passed. We were really worried about Thao Dam on that last physical exam, but by then, it felt like everybody was pulling for him, and he made it. We were relieved. Happy . . . it was over!"

When the ribbon was cut, officially and ceremoniously opening the East Dallas Community Police and Refugees Affairs Office in December of 1985, it was staffed by Corporal Ron Cowart, PSOs Thai, Keovilay, and Dam, as well as a rotating team of volunteers. The sign in the window that announced it as the East Dallas Storefront was in triplicate—in three different languages. Inside, there was a small waiting area near the door of the station, furnished with a battered couch and a few molded plastic chairs. A counter running halfway across the room separated this area from the desks of the officers.

The walls of the Peak Street shop space, freshly painted, were covered by flags. In an attempt to represent every homeland of every community resident, the decor has become its own style—"early United Nations."

The Cambodian Flag with the temple, Angkor Wat, in its center, the Vietnamese Flag, the Laotian Flag, the Mexican Flag, the Taiwanese Flag, the Salvadorean Flag, the royal-blue flag of the Cambodian Lions' Club (the *first* Cambodian Lions' Club), the state flag of Texas and the American Stars and Stripes all share space on the storefront walls.

The PSOs desks were positioned in the front. Corporal Cowart's desk was in the rear corner, overseeing the entire space. When the parade of mostly Asian people began filing in through the door, the faces they found waiting for them were friendly. Leck, Thao, and Paul were ready and able to speak the community residents' language and help them attend to their needs.

In the back room, there were a few more desks as well as the rice storeroom, a few more closets and a functional, if not congenial, bathroom. The desks and tables could be pushed together to serve as a conference table or be separated into the layout of a makeshift study hall for the Asian students,

Explorer Scouts and Girl Scouts who the staff encouraged to drop in after school to do homework.

As the older people left the storefront, holding their bag of rice and a loaf of bread donated from a Dallas bakery, they would bow and thank the PSOs and always show their appreciation to Ron Cowart. Paul says, "Everyone was always grateful and especially grateful to Ronny. Everyone always wants to bow to Ronny!"

This may be because Ronny always bows back. From the beginning, Cowart saw this as an exchange of cultural values, as a learning experience for him as well as a teaching experience. Fully comfortable slipping off his shoes upon entering an Asian household, and fully comfortable bowing and greeting the community elders by pressing his palms together and saying *chumriap sua,* Ronny won the hearts of the community. Paul says simply, "All of the Asian people know that Ronny loves them. So they love Ronny."

And how does all this love translate into police work?

Paul and Ron maintain that it is the essential element. It is the essence of community police work, which is what the storefront attempts to put into practice. It is a far cry from the glamorized violence of television cops . . . it is probably more akin to the stereotypical fifties image of friendly Officer Bob helping schoolchildren cross the street. A crucial difference here is that the streets that must be crossed in the nineties hold many more hazards than errant traffic.

Those police and police supporters who oppose the idea of a storefront, particularly one such as the East Dallas Storefront in Little Asia, one that openly hands out food and offers help in getting social service assistance, maintain that giving *some* help is a fine idea, although it shouldn't necessarily be done by the police department and, most importantly, it shouldn't be done for an indefinite period of time. There are those, both within the police department and taxpayers on the outside of the department, who feel that once the refugees have been helped for a time, they should be progressing, moving onward and upward, out of the welfare loop, and finally, moving out of Little Asia and into a better neighborhood. If the refugees are given support through the storefront, will they ever find a better life, will they leave the neighborhood?

It becomes an interesting question, one that has arisen many times before with other types of social service programs, and one that has been debated many times. Does an agency like the storefront encourage dependence rather than independence? Or at least, it sounds as if it is that question, that same liberal we-have-to-help-these-people-argument versus the conservative yes-but-then-we-have-to-stand-back-and-let-these-people-pull-themselves-up-by-their-own-bootstraps stance.

But Paul Thai sees the situation in Little Asia as its own separate world, with its own problems. "When we walked the beat in the early days of the storefront," Paul remembers, "we saw terrible problems. We would go into apartments and there would be children who were so hungry, starving. I would open the refrigerator and there would be no food. Nothing in there.

"I remember this one little girl, looking at me, so hungry. We went to the store and bought food and brought it back. I gave this little girl a banana and she ate it so fast. I gave her another one and it disappeared. Then another one. She ate three great big bananas in seconds. I felt like crying, seeing her eat like that. The problem? The family had no money. They couldn't speak English, they didn't know how to get assistance, get food stamps. They couldn't find an office, fill out a form, understand the process. They are starting here in America from so far behind.

"Then there was an old Cambodian man who needed someone to translate for him at the welfare office, so I went with him. There was a young pretty woman who was the social worker, and she sat with her legs crossed. This is a sign of disrespect—showing the bottoms of your feet and pointing them at someone. But this is America, so I keep the old man calm about this. Then the man had difficulty understanding some of the questions so he would give a wrong answer and she would write it down, then it would have to be changed, so she would pull out a new form. It was frustrating. I'm sure for her, but for us, too. Anyway, she wadded up these forms that were ruined and threw them over the old man's head into the wastebasket. He was furious, stood up and said we had to leave. She had interfered with his spirits, the thirty-two spirits that keep him in harmony, by throwing that garbage over his head. The head is a sacred place. He couldn't stay there. So we got up and left the office. With no food stamps for the old man.

"Another story is this. There was a woman who lost her husband to the Khmer Rouge in Cambodia and I don't know how many others in her family, but she came here to Dallas, to Little Asia, with four sons. The oldest son was good and he worked hard to make enough money to support the family, to keep his younger brothers in school, but it was still not enough. They were still always hungry. One day, two of the younger sons got into a fight, a terrible fight. You will not believe what they fought over. It was a bowl of rice. They were both hungry and they fought over a bowl of rice and the younger one took a knife and stabbed his brother. He was sorry and started crying and called the police and the ambulance came, but it was too late. That son died. And the other son was taken away to a juvenile home. Then, the oldest son, the number one son, got a second job as a roofer. We don't know how it happened, but he fell off the roof where he was working and he died. So number three son killed number two son and now number one son is dead, too. We went to see the mother, who was in very bad shape, and Ron asked her how she felt about America now. And you know what she said, after all this happened? 'America is good. It is my luck that is bad.' "

The Asians who are beginning new lives in East Dallas, particularly the Cambodians, are not starting from scratch. They are starting from way before scratch. No language, no resources, no support, no recognizable signs, no money, no food, no history, and without the cultural makeup that would enable them to ask for it, no help. For the family with no food in the refrigerator, weak with hunger and dizzied by the newness of life in America, bootstraps to pull themselves up by will be a long time coming.

The cultural differences that are embedded in spiritual and formally religious beliefs are so deep that there is little vocabulary adequate to describe or discuss them. When Paul is asked why he didn't explain to the young social worker that her action was offensive to the old man, his answer is simple. "If I were speaking to a civic group or if I were giving a speech in a school about cultural differences, I would explain that, of course. But I have fears sometimes that if I were to explain to a social worker in a situation like that, that the head is sacred and that there are thirty-two spirits there, she would turn on me and say, 'But this is America now—you are in America now,' and the old man wouldn't be any better off and she would be even madder." And although Paul doesn't explain it himself, it is clear that because of his youth in relation to the old man he was helping, it would have been another layer of offense and shame for the old man if Paul had made a defense and the argument had escalated. The most respectful path for Paul to take, both to the elder Cambodian and to the young American, was the one that led out the door.

The Cambodian woman who lost her sons is unable to criticize America, unable to place blame. She is culturally unable to complain that she needed more help, that her sons needed counseling, that they needed financial assistance, that her boys were unable to cope with American high school, with American customs, with the lack of friendship, of connection to the world in which they found themselves living. She was unable to say that they needed spiritual or mental or emotional counseling. This is not to suggest that there is any real single villain to blame—it simply illustrates her need to take on the suffering. As Ron Cowart explains again and again in his speeches and seminars on cultural differences, the Asians expect to suffer, would never consider public grieving, or asking for sympathy or assistance. Do they need it? Yes. But for the Americans who want to help, a whole new vocabulary, common ground, has to be established.

So when a cop or a critic suggests that it is inappropriate to give bags of rice away to families where two adults work at steady jobs, have even managed to buy a nice-looking used van, Paul shakes his head. Paul always tries to give the rice. "It is not that we are giving them only food. The rice is a symbol of friendship, of American friendship. It will not make them stop working or think they can depend on handouts. Nobody wants a handout, they want a helping hand."

The idea of helping the refugees help themselves to get on their feet and move along, up the ladder, to a better neighborhood, and to a more materially managable American way of life is not a cruel or unusual plan. It is not unlike Charles Kemp's analogy of using the triage method in helping the Little Asia community. One should treat the neediest, the one who is suffering the most seriously, then move on to the next neediest. However, as Paul and Ron and Charles Kemp would say, this is not the same goal-oriented, progressive, American-dreaming community that most American-born Americans either grew up in, recognize through television and popular songs, or aspire to.

This is a community made up of refugees who feel that America means life. To ask for more than life, more than a place to breathe freely without fear, might make the refugees seem greedy, might make them sound ungrateful. And there are no refugees who endured the Khmer Rouge, the border camps, the devastation of their own homelands who are ungrateful to be in America. Paul repeats over and over that, for almost everyone, "America was the dream. America is the dream."

Paul and his family were not the only Cambodians who thought it would be better to get across the border into Thailand. Moving farther and farther West was every refugee's goal. This time, though, when the Thai family risked their lives to escape, Paul was able to tell them the name of the place that they were headed . . . Khao I Dang camp.

"Our second time on the Cambodian side of the border, our second escape, we found the same thing. Not enough food, no money, no work, so some of my brothers and I started smuggling again. We sneaked back and forth across the Thai border. But this one time, the Thai soldiers caught us and were going to kill us. They had us—Mao, Tang, and me—along with many others in a truck and were taking us away and we knew we were going to die. So Mao and some others jumped off and began running. The soldiers shot at them and we weren't sure whether Mao made it safely away or not. What Tang and I did know for sure was that we were dead. But an American Red Cross truck drove by us and we started screaming and yelling, making signs and acting out so he would understand that they were going to murder us. We begged them to follow the truck. And you know what? They did. They followed us for a long time until I guess the Thai soldiers gave up that they would be able to just take us off and kill us, so they brought us to Khao I Dang camp.

"They gave us food there. More food than we had seen in a long time. We liked it there, but we missed our families and knew our families would think we were dead. So the next day, they took us back to the border to our families.

"My mother was sure we had been killed because Mao had gotten safely away when we were caught and he had gone back and told her that Tang and Pov were going to be killed. In our culture, we burn paper money when someone dies and my mother had already burned money for us!"

Paul was happy to be reunited with his family, but even happier to be able to tell them about the Khao I Dang camp. He and Tang described the kind faces of the American Red Cross workers and perhaps more importantly, they described the food they had been given to eat, its taste, and its relative bounty. They had known before that they needed to cross the border into Thailand, but they now knew the name of the place they needed to go.

"My father had a little piece of gold to bribe one of the Thai soldiers who guarded the border. The only problem with bribing one soldier was that the other soldiers didn't know about the bribe, so as we ran into Thailand just before dawn one morning, we still got shot at. We made it across the border though and there was the American Red Cross bus waiting to take us to Khao I Dang."

When the refugees were accepted as *legal* refugees, they were assigned tracing numbers . . . what Paul and his family referred to as T-numbers. That was their identification and proved that they belonged in a specific camp. *Belonging* in Khao I Dang was each refugee's goal. It was a necessary stop on the way West. Every Cambodian refugee can tell stories about hiding in Khao I Dang—either from the perspective of one who hid or one who helped others to hide.

A Cambodian woman now living in Chicago, Illinois, tells of lying in a shallow grave under the makeshift floorboards in a refugee hut during daylight. This was her hiding place and her home until she was able to find a family member or a sponsor who would give her legal refugee status.

And those illegal refugees that were unable to find legal status? "Many people died there, with no number, no name. But Khao I Dang was the camp where refugees started toward America, so people took the risks to get there," Paul says. Once there, the refugees' hunger was somewhat appeased, but other problems multiplied.

After a 1989 visit to the Site 2 camp on the Thai border where the Cambodians still living have been classified as displaced persons rather than as refugees, writer Margaret Drabble, in an article for *Harper's* Magazine, referred to the camp not as the Killing Fields, but as the fields of Killing Time. She watched these people, victims of the battle between the Vietnamese, the Cambodian Freedom Fighters, and the still-active Khmer Rouge, mired in poverty, red tape, and boredom. There is little energy, little hope that things will change. People will be born and will die in the Site 2 camp, displaced, on the border, with no country, no culture.

There was daily on-the-job training at the storefront. No one knew who would walk through the door bringing a truckload of donated clothing, food, toys, and books, and no one could anticipate the needs of a shy Asian woman who would slip in quietly and stand in the corner, eyes down, until one of the PSOs determined her language, her problems, her needs. Paul, Leck, and Thao were constantly in and out the door, taking people to the welfare office, helping them fill out the applications, the government forms, the requests for assistance. They were asked by families to mediate in the schools and between family members themselves. When the neighborhood children began filling up the office after school, the PSOs became homework tutors. They were advisors, counselors, listeners, friends, and, as they hefted the five-pound bags of rice over the counter, providers.

And cops. Periodically, they stood up and put on their hats and headed out to the streets. Paul laughs about going on patrol in the early days. "Ronny would call a community meeting to talk about crime prevention and we would all be going to translate into the necessary languages. Ronny would walk out the door, then Thao would follow him, then Leck would follow Thao, then I would follow Leck. Ronny would say to us to come up and walk with him and we would say yes, but pretty soon we would be all stretched out in a line again. Cultural differences! We would be showing respect to each other by allowing the oldest to go first, then the most respect to Ronny, allowing him to walk in front of all of us, but he would say that he felt like a mother duck!"

On patrol, Ron Cowart and the Asian PSOs would knock on doors, introduce themselves and try to find out what they could do to help the area residents. Paul says that many people were hungry, so, "We got them food." Many people were isolated, so, "We asked them to come and see us at the storefront, told them that we would be there for them, would help them get jobs, fill out forms." Many people were rapidly getting lost in the system, so, "We would go with them to the agencies and translate for them when they needed welfare or food stamps." Many people were sick, so "We would take them for medical care."

In addition to providing these immediate services and introducing themselves, in addition to making friends in the community, Paul explains that they were laying another kind of groundwork in Little Asia. "When we talked to people about their needs, we also asked them if people were bothering them. We asked if they saw other people, their neighbors, being bothered by others. We asked if they saw people stealing or acting funny. We asked about cars parked in the neighborhood, who they belonged to, how long they had been there. We asked people to tell us about anything unusual that they heard or saw."

Another job that Paul found himself taking on was that of truant officer. When he saw school-age children on the street or in the home during what should have been class time for them, he asked questions, even though he already knew the answers. "Sometimes we would see kids, maybe eight or nine years old, staying home to take care of the babies in the family while the parents were out working.

"This would make me so mad, because I want to see kids in school. Sometimes, when I would say this to the parents, they would tell me that was their business and not my business, but it is my business. It might not be my family, but I still want to see every kid, not just Cambodian, but the Laotian and the Vietnamese kids, too, in school every day because it is unfair to the kids to make them stay home. The parents would say to me that it is for all the kids' sakes that they make the oldest one stay home, so the parents can go to work and earn money to buy the food and pay the rent.

"But it is not fair. I firmly believe that if you make your oldest child stay home and care for the others while you work, that oldest kid is going to grow up without education and find out that the reason was because he or she had to stay home and baby-sit. Then, that oldest kid is going to be very angry, very mad at you, the parents."

Paul says all this with quiet conviction and adds, "Sometimes I get really angry myself with the parents. I don't show it. I talk nicely to them. But I tell them that the children are their future. I tell them, yes, you are earning money now, but since most us don't speak English, you are going to have to depend on your children. You are going to have to depend on their education. I understand the financial problems of *now,* but I try to convince them to think about the future. I, myself, would rather suffer now for later. I like to take the hard knocks now and have fun later.

"I tell them to worry about the future, especially for the kids. After all, I remind them, this is America, not Cambodia. In Cambodia, you didn't have to worry about learning a new language, about learning to speak English. You didn't have to worry so much about education, you could always find something to do. But not in America. Here, the other kids will look down on your kids if they don't speak English, if they don't have much education. And here, you won't be able to say you didn't have a chance. This is America, the land of opportunity. You have to grab your chance!"

Paul's passion for education, about American opportunities, remains quiet and contained. And despite his optimism about the future, his faith that life in America can be one of freedom, education, and advancement, particularly for the children, he remains sympathetic to those parents he chastises.

"The parents have a difficult time. The whole family, and Cambodian families are normally big ones—seven or eight kids—usually just has one room to stay in. Most of the time, the family stays home because they have no money to spend and no English to speak. The apartment is small and there is no room for the children to play. Nobody can move.

"The children have no toys. Sometimes, kindhearted people donate toys for the children, but they disappear from the storefront quickly. Some parents don't even bother to take one toy because they know they have seven children at home and it wouldn't be fair to bring home one toy that one child would be able to play with."

Nearly all of the existing literature on raising children speaks of the need children have to play. Toys are referred to by most child development experts as the tools of childhood. Play is called the work of childhood.

Paul shakes his head when he talks about the families and their problems. With all the instincts of a good parent, he knows that the children need to play, need toys. He knows that they need to be children before they can be care givers themselves. On the other hand, Paul knows that there is a generation of Cambodian parents who had no childhood, who had only the Khmer Rouge soldiers pointing real weapons at them, forcing them to pick up real tools and labor in real work camps. So while magazine articles in so-called women's or parents' magazines stress the value of play and the value of quality time, Paul acknowledges that those concepts might be a generation or so away.

"Although," Paul smiles, "I have always wanted my children to have something at Christmastime, like other American children. So a few years ago, Marina and I bought them some new clothes that they needed and we wrapped the packages all up for Christmas. Well, the kids found the boxes in the closet a few days before Christmas and opened them up. And even put the clothes on and wore them all day! So at night, when they took the clothes off, even though Marina laughed at me about this, I folded them all up and put them back in the boxes and wrapped them up again and put them under the tree that some friends from the department, Sergeant Parker and Corporal Dorsey, brought over. We couldn't afford to get more presents and I was determined that they would have those boxes to open on Christmas morning."

Paul knows that he is torn between the East and West when it comes to raising his children. "In Cambodian families, the parents don't ask the children what they think about things or how they feel about things. Parents make the decisions. Unless the grandparents are living. My grandparents were already dead when I was growing up, but in many households, the grandparents are there, and they make the rules. For example, if a father wants to punish his son for something, the grandfather can step in and say no, he can stop *his* son from punishing *his* grandson. And the children have no say so, they are supposed to speak only when spoken to.

"But with my son, Chetra, I think it will be different. I want to hear his opinion on things. If he has something good to say, I will listen." And does

Paul feel the same about his daughter, Somaly, who was born in 1986? "I want both my children to have an education and to speak English. I think Chet will have an easier time getting a job, I think there are more things he can do as a boy. With Maly, I hope she will go to school and be a teacher. My dream for me at one time," Paul says thoughtfully. "There are many things about America that I think are better than the Cambodian way. My parents never said, in words, that they loved me. Cambodian parents just don't say that to their children the way American parents do, even though they do love them very much. I think with my children we will mix the American way with the Cambodian."

Believing strongly that the children are the future, Paul wants to see them educated, English-speaking, and success oriented. But he also wants them to have fun. That's why, in 1986, Paul Thai, Cambodian PSO for the Dallas Police Department became Paul Thai, Girl Scout Leader. Paul shakes his head and makes a face: "That was something! Me with the girl scout troup!"

Troop 410, like Ron Cowart's Explorer Troop, met at the storefront. Paul, assisted by two young women, nursing students of Charles Kemp, were the leaders. The thirteen to seventeen girls were mostly Cambodian, but there were a few Laotian and Hispanic girls who joined Troop 410, too. "We didn't worry much about the badges of the Girl Scouts. We mostly took them places for fun. They had no way of getting out of the neighborhood. Parents were working or had no cars to take them, so after school, and on weekends, we would take them to amusement parks and skating. We would plan activities for them. I remember one awful time when we tried to take them swimming!

"We made arrangements at the YWCA for all of the girls to go swimming and they were so excited. They all said, yeah, yeah, we love to swim, so I took everyone and we were all at the front desk, and I pointed out where they should go and change, and they all looked at me and started crying. They didn't want to wear bathing suits. They were from traditional Cambodian families and they would never show their legs in a bathing suit. You see, Cambodian women never show the upper part of the leg, and these girls were so upset. They wanted to swim, but they thought they would be able to leave all their clothes on. We left the Y pretty fast that day."

The girls scout troop is now supervised by some American friends, Ron and Shirley Decker, but Paul is quick to identify girls walking home from school or from the store as one of "his girl scouts."

In addition to the scout troops, the storefront staff started a soccer league and tried to organize a baseball league. The baseball league presented some problems for Paul who had no idea of how to play, what the rules were, or what the point was. "I still don't," Paul says ruefully, "but we did win a few games anyway. The teams we played didn't understand the game either!" Providing group activities for the young people in the neighborhood was not merely another example of the selfless community service performed by Cowart, the other storefront cops, and the PSOs. It was also police work. Preventative police work.

The young people in the neighborhood, the future of the Cambodians as Paul was always reminding their parents, were and still are at constant risk. Although many Cambodian adolescents were quick to pick up American teenage fads and fashions, it was not easy for them to slip into the normal high school or junior high school crowd and become a part of the scene. The Asian students looked different and sounded different. The best English-speaking Cambodian teen was still going to have an accent, still going to misunderstand colloquialisms, and find daily teenage jargon peppered with references to television, music, film, and other shared popular cultural history impossible to follow. The American teens' lack of knowledge or understanding of where the Asian teens came from, what their life had been like before the United States was also a barrier.

If a Cambodian girl did make the attempt to fit in, styled her hair in an American way, wore makeup, talked loudly and dressed in a casual American style, she would be risking her own family ties. Paul often points out teenagers who change their appearance to be more Americanized on their way to school, then try to change it back to being Cambodian on their way home. In addition to the stress of keeping up two appearances, the girl must keep up with her schoolwork, both for her own sake and for the honor of the family, and she has to help with the care of the younger children since both her parents are out working.

Because of this pressure and because the Asian family is traditionally not one to sit down and encourage heart-to-heart, tell-all discussions, the children are often isolated, often lack any kind of one-to-one guidance. School counselors are, of course, available, but to seek out a virtual stranger and discuss personal problems with him or her would be impossible for an Asian teenager. In their homelands, these teenagers would not be faced with the kind of hard choices, the challenges or the stresses that American life presents. Here, they are very often troubled and alone with their problems. This is what puts them at such high risk for gang recruitment. And this is why the storefront tries so hard to present alternatives to the gangs that are watching and waiting to snag these pressured children.

Paul is especially concerned with keeping children in school and out of this kind of trouble. "Kids talk to me all the time about the trouble they have in school. Teachers think they are smart Asians and expect them to do well, and they are lost. They are not understanding anything. I picked up one boy who was playing hooky and brought him back to school. Two times I found this boy. And he told me he wanted an education, he wanted to go to school, but he was lost there. He said he came to America when he was thirteen or fourteen and was placed in school, and didn't understand anything that was being said. He had never been in school, he had been in the camps and before that, had worked under the Khmer Rouge. Now he was in school and was lost. So the school officials told him that there was a rap session after school for kids having problems and that he was supposed to go. He went and there were no translators so he couldn't understand anything. He says he loves school, but he cannot stay there. Cannot be so different there.

"So what if someone comes up to him and says, 'I know how you feel, I know just how you feel. Here, have a cigarette, or have something to drink or eat, I'll buy you a meal?' And this person speaks his language and is nice and understands his problems with his school and with his family? This person is going to start having some influence over this kid. And this person is going to be able to persuade this kid to join a gang.

"That is how it happens. One-on-one. In Asian families, either there is no time for families to talk or else families are uncomfortable talking in a certain direct manner, so there is no one to talk to this kid, no one to express a personal interest. That is why the Explorers are important. Because Ronny cares about each kid. That is why it is so important for the storefront to be there, and for us to get to know everyone. So there is a personal connection.

"It's very similar to converting to Christianity. In the refugee camps, when the ministers would come and talk to the Asians, would show some interest in one person, that was something we had never experienced. The monk is a spiritual guide, but is not a counselor, not directly one-on-one. That is why the ministers who go door to door, who talk to Asians personally, one-on-one, are so successful at converting Asians to their church. Because the people think, ah . . . here is someone who really cares about me."

On Friday evenings in the Little Asia neighborhood, Mormon missionaries still visit door to door in the apartment complexes where Cambodian families live. Every week, they knock on Paul's door. Paul shrugs his shoulders when he invites them in and explains quietly that he has already told them he is a Baptist, but they keep visiting anyway. Marina hands them a glass of Coke with ice and they settle in quietly and observe the scene. A few of Paul's neighbors are visiting and when an older man, one of the respected elders in the building, in the entire community, begins a long story of fighting the Khmer Rouge and the Vietnamese, he makes a joke. Paul laughs as he translates it for those who don't speak Khmer, but the missionaries are already laughing. They speak the Cambodian language, Khmer, fluently. Paul nods toward them and says this is why they are successful missionaries. They speak the language, they try to understand the culture, and, most importantly, they interact one-on-one in the Cambodian community.

In gang recruitment, the promise of material wealth, of having more spending money, of being able to follow fads and fashion, is held out as bait, but it is a hollow promise for the kids who succumb to the temptation. The world of the gang, by necessity, must remain private, must be one where membership is essential. Because of the illegal activities encouraged and demanded, the world remains a shadowy, secretive one. And the youths who join remain on the fringes of teenage society. But for the Asian teens who are beyond even those fringes, the gang still holds the attraction of providing friends and a sense of belonging. And it is those teens caught between East and West, trying so hard to belong—somewhere—who are among the first to become engulfed in the rising tide of urban street crime.

6

And Robbers

We just know the name of democracy, not the details.
    —Chea Sokha, a resident of Site 2 camp, Thailand

Paul Thai, Leck Keovilay, Thao Dam, and Ron Cowart believed that their presence would empower the neighborhood residents. The storefront, staffed with people who spoke their languages and understood their gestures, would enable them all to work together to resist being easy victims of crime and violence.

That was the plan . . . crime fighting through prevention as well as intervention. A typical day for Paul, Leck, and Thao might include some paperwork, some translation of forms, a trip to the food stamps office with some Little Asia applicants, a community meeting in an apartment building where Ron Cowart, through his PSOs, explained the most basic of crime-prevention tips—keep your doors locked, don't let anyone in you house if you don't know them, report suspicious-looking people and vehicles in your neighborhood. Since the community he was addressing had come primarily from the refugee camps and had had no control over their former living situation, the most basic advice—don't let anyone in your house—was essential. The Cambodian refugees had been powerless to stop anyone from searching and looting their makeshift homes in the camps. Surely they were not going to allow themselves to talk back to Americans—even American criminals.

"Sometimes," remembers Paul, "when we went on foot patrol and visited a building where mostly Cambodians lived, a family, smiling, might let us in the door. We would bow and greet them and they would bow and greet us. They would keep smiling, even though we could look around and see that there was not much to smile about. Maybe we would hear the water in the toilet running, and maybe it would be real hot—the air conditioner would be broken. But still, the family would give us a cold drink and keep saying that everything was fine. Ron would be after me to talk to them, to get them to open up about any complaints they might have, so I would continue to inquire. And then," Paul smiles, "they would say something that was all wrapped up in kind words about the United States, you know, about how they didn't want to complain because all the Americans had been so good to them, but the air conditioner had never worked and the children couldn't sleep at night because of the heat.

"Then, they would say to me softly, 'we tell *you* this, but don't tell him,' and they would gesture toward Ronny. I would explain to them that he was their friend and that he wanted to help them. And they would agree. They knew he was their friend and they believed that he was sincere. But he was an American and America had opened its arms to the refugees and they did not want to complain to an American. They never wanted to seem ungrateful.

"I would explain over and over on these visits that it was Ronny's job to help them and it was my job to help Ronny to do his job and this would go on for a while until finally I would be given permission to translate what was going on for Ronny." Paul laughs when he remembers Ronny looking back and forth. "Ronny would be saying, 'what's he saying, what's he saying' while I was trying to get our host to let me tell him something!"

An American might believe the old adage that the squeaky wheel gets the grease, but it would be difficult to convince a Cambodian refugee that a complaint from him or her—no matter how legitimate—would bring help. Many Cambodians, even those who have been here for several years, harbor a deep fear of being sent back to their country. They feel that any complaint, any criticism of the treatment they receive here in America might be cause for deportation. Even if they have never said it themselves, there are few Americans who have never heard the muttered, under-the-breath phrase—"if they don't like it here, why don't they go back where they came from" or a variation thereof. Every immigrant and every refugee has heard—and feared—that muttering, too.

Not only does this silent acceptance on the part of the refugees make it difficult to help them with housing problems, health problems, and their psychological needs, it also invites abuse by those who see refugees as easy marks.

"When we had been here about a year and a half, we went to buy our first car," says Paul. "My brother was learning to drive then, but none of us had a license yet, so a Cambodian friend who had been here a long time took us to the dealer. We were so proud of that first car! It was a Ford Grenada, a 1976 model. We bought it in 1983, financed it on time payments, for forty-five hundred dollars." Paul shakes his head and laughs. "A little while after we bought, we saw someone with the very same car, same make and model, and asked them what they paid for their car and they told us $2,000. We thought that meant that their car was junk and that our car was superior!

"We didn't think that for very long though. The next day, after we bought our car, it didn't start. We finally got it going and took it back and they looked at it and shook their heads and said, 'too bad, no warranty.' They said we had bought the car 'as is.' We had a translator with us and they told him to tell us to look at the paper we had signed, that we had no warranty, and the translator looked and told us that there was nothing we could do because we had signed the paper.

"So we had them fix it—there was nothing else we could do. They said there was something wrong with one part and they fixed it and charged us about two hundred dollars. Then after we got it home, it wouldn't start. So they came and checked it and they couldn't start it either. So we said they should fix it this time for free because they had just fixed it and it was broken already, but they said no, now it was a different part that was broken. So we had to pay more again to get it fixed and it was going to cost about $120 this time.

"My father, my brother, and I all looked at each other. We were all thinking what are we going to do? My father finally said that they should go ahead and fix it. But none of us understood how they could fix one thing and then the other thing could break so fast. So they took it in and fixed it.

"It broke again. And again and again! It was just like in a movie—like with clowns going around and around in circles. And every time the mechanic would say he was sorry, but it was our car—it was too old. And my brother, Bun Thai, got so mad. His face turned red and he started waving all the receipts we had from all the times we had it fixed. And he waved them and waved them, saying, 'Look at this, look at this!' He couldn't speak English, but he told us later that he was so mad, that the English came into his head and he started shouting, 'Money, money, I gave you money!' So the guy got scared and got the manager who came and tried to be calm and professional and said he was sorry, but the car was too old, but Bun just kept shouting, 'Fix it, fix it!' Finally, the manager told someone to come over and fix it. I think he wanted to get us out of there. That time, the car lasted about a week before it broke again. Then we traded it away, still paying on it, and got a Buick Regal.

"We loved that Buick. It was a great car. A friend of ours came over and we told him about our car troubles and he said, in Cambodian, do you know what FORD stands for? The F stands for FIX, the O stands for OR, the R stands for REPAIR, and the D stands for DAILY. FIX OR REPAIR DAILY, he said in Cambodian! We said, 'wow' and went around telling everyone not to buy Fords! Having that car was just like having an ox cart.

"It wasn't just the American car dealer or the garage, though, that took advantage. The Cambodian friend who had taken us there in the first place had been in America a long time and he got a commission on the Ford Grenada that we bought. So he took advantage, too, I think. Almost all the Cambodians in East Dallas went to that used car dealer, so we learned to tell people not to buy cars from Mario's Auto Sales. And I said, especially not Ford Grenadas!"

Car dealers shouldn't be singled out as the only ones who saw the refugees coming. Paul is sure that those who knew that the Asians loved to bargain figured out a way to make a bigger profit, too. "Whenever we went to the flea market in Dallas, we loved it, because it reminded us of the market in Cambodia. And we could bargain—we loved that. We would go up to a stall and ask how much a chicken was and the guy would say ten dollars and we would say, 'Come on, give it to us for seven dollars,' and he would finally say, 'Okay,' and then we would feel real proud of ourselves, getting the chicken for seven dollars.

"We would feel good about our bargain until someone would tell us that the chicken only cost three dollars! Same chicken that we paid seven dollars for—after bargaining! It felt like either way we lost. And if we complained, we knew what we would hear—'If you don't like it here, why don't you go back to China?' Or Japan or wherever else they could think of. I heard that many times myself."

Although in his first years in America, Paul found it nearly impossible to complain for himself, he learned to complain for others. When Ron Cowart and PSO Paul Thai visited a Cambodian family who Paul could finally persuade to talk about the conditions of their apartment and who would allow him to tell Ron about it, Paul found that being an advocate for others suited him.

"We called in the authorities to come out and write many citations to landlords and building owners in those days," Paul remembers. "We made a lot of enemies, I think.

"We learned, though, that we had to walk a fine line. People wanted us to be very careful in our complaints, not only because it was natural for them not to want to complain, but also because they knew they might get put out on the street. You see, many buildings would never allow so many people in one apartment. Cambodians often have very big families and sometimes more than one family wants to live together. And these were buildings where the landlord was allowing as many as seven all the way up to sixteen people to live in a one-bedroom apartment. If the landlord or the owner got too many citations, he might just sell the building and go out of the residential business."

Paul learned to be a community advocate, albeit a cautious one, and also, as part of his on-the-job training, he learned to be a family counselor.

Domestic disputes and incidences of family violence were frequent neighborhood complaints. The isolation and poverty in which most of the families lived as well as the frustration over some of their present living conditions, conditions about which they felt helpless to change, contributed to the household disturbances that Ron and the PSOs were called to investigate. But cultural differences, too, proved to be at the heart of many of these calls. Paul, not in any way defending violence, explains quite simply, "There is no law against child abuse in Cambodia. People beat their children because they love them, want to discipline them."

In America, the variety of options available to children provides more ready temptation to disobey, to go against family rules and parents who might not have had occasion to raise their hands against their children in their own homeland find themselves frustrated by their rapidly changing children, and find themselves fighting a looseness of behavior that was simply never witnessed before. Paul often found himself not only mediating between parent and child, and husband and wife, but also between America and Cambodia. He explained the customs, the behavioral differences, and the opportunities the children would have if they were allowed to study and go to school, and he explained how much more readily their children would learn if they were allowed to assimilate, if they were allowed to be Cambodian–American. And he explained to Cambodian parents that beating their children was against the law.

And he also explained to Cambodian husbands that their wives, too, were protected by the law. "I think we put many families back together," says Paul. "I'm not sure it was always the way that the police department would have normally handled everything. We tried not to put people in jail—we tried to put them back together instead."

Early in 1986, only a few months after the storefront officially opened its doors, Cowart and the Asian PSOs, already tested daily as advocates and counselors, got their chance to prove themselves as cops.

In late January, seven Cambodian refugees were robbed by five men who forced their way into the refugees' Little Asia apartment. The robbers, carrying what appeared to be machine guns, tied up the Cambodians, ransacked the apartment, took the television, stereo, jewelry, and cash. Those were the bare facts that were reported in the newspapers. What could not be printed as fact was the confused report that the robbers were Asian, sporting New Wave hairstyles that mystified and scared their victims. They looked frightening, they talked tough, and to the already skittish Cambodians, their presence in the Asian neighborhoods was terrifying.

This was one in a string of robberies that had been plaguing the Dallas area. New Southeast Asian refugees were the most common prey—both the refugees who lived in Little Asia and others who lived in smaller clusters throughout the Dallas area. Crime had been escalating, and with the report of automatic weapons being used in this holdup, there was the suspicion that organized crime had become involved.

Because the robbers were identified as Asians and the victims were Asians, Ron Cowart and the PSOs hit the streets. They patrolled the Little Asia neighborhood, acting as both questioners and listeners. They felt sure that people in the neighborhood could give them the information they needed in order to identify and catch this gang, but they needed to be patient and persistent as they canvassed the area. The residents were frightened by the gang of criminals, by the stories they had heard, the threats that had been repeated throughout the community. The residents were learning to trust the storefront police, but it was a slow process. Paul, Leck, and Thao visited door-to-door, making themselves known, asking questions, performing various tasks for the residents so they would know that the PSOs were sincere in their offers of friendship, help, and protection.

The Cambodian couple who had been tied up and robbed had given thorough descriptions not only of the robbers, but also of the stolen goods. Paul remembers the report distinctly. "They knew it was a Seiko watch that had been taken. And they described their stereo equipment very well. They gave us the brand name—Lasonic—but even more important for our purposes, they described a small dent on the front of it."

Finally, the Dallas Police department received a tip. An Asian who had been a robbery victim heard from someone else where the robbers lived. He, in turn, called the police and reported the address—4411 Roseland Avenue, just about eight blocks from the storefront. Acting on this tip, a police officer visited the storefront to speak with Thao Dam who would act as the Vietnamese interpreter on the case. When this officer arrived to speak to Dam, a Vietnamese woman was in the storefront, reporting that she had been robbed at gun and knife point by a man whose car she had seen parked at the same Roseland Avenue address.

Calls were made. Backup arrived. Someone had to stay at the storefront, so it was arranged that Leck Keovilay would remain there, monitoring the radio, prepared to call in more help if necessary. Ron Cowart, Paul Thai, Thao Dam and several other Dallas police Department officers proceeded to 4411 Roseland Avenue.

The suspected robbers had been identified as Vietnamese which meant that Thao Dam would go to the front door to translate. He accompanied three other officers into the building. Ron Cowart and Paul Thai went around to the back of the building. Although there was no rear entrance, there was a small terrace off the second floor window in the apartment where they suspected the gang was staying. Paul doesn't remember fear, but recalls being excited. "It was the first time. For Leck and Thao and me, this was exciting business. Ron had made a lot of arrests, so I don't think it felt new to him," Paul says, "although it was a kind of first for him—Asian robbers instead of American ones.

"Ronny and I waited in back, then we heard some noise. Someone shouted, 'Police!' then we heard a lot more noise. Two guys burst out of the terrace door and jumped, but they landed on a part of the roof. Ronny drew his gun and identified us as the police and told them to lie down. I didn't have a gun to draw, so I drew my baton, my nightstick, and Ronny and I stood there, ready.

"The two guys just looked at Ronny and shook their heads. They climbed back into the apartment through the terrace window. So we went in then, and there were nine of them inside the apartment. They had wild, mean-looking hairstyles—real punk looking—and they talked real tough. They acted like they knew the system and they weren't afraid. One man and one girl spoke some English—more and better than the rest of them. Thao Dam talked and talked, translating and giving them their rights. I didn't understand anything because I didn't speak Vietnamese. Then we gathered them all together—the officers had their weapons drawn and Thao and I had our batons raised—and we started to search the apartment.

"We found so much stuff. Piles of car stereos, jewelry, all kinds of equipment. The most exciting find was a Seiko watch and a Lasonic stereo. Most exciting because the stereo had a dent in it, right where the description said it was supposed to be.

"After we talked to them and searched the apartment we had to transport them downtown. Some of them looked at me and said something about me being Asian and asked what I was doing with the police. They said I joined the wrong side, the other side, and they were going to come back and get me. Before I joined the police department, I really feared these kinds of gangs, but now I was seeing them up close. They were people just like me. All together, they were showing off, showing their teeth, but you could tell it was an act. They were showing off for each other. When we got them apart, they started talking real softly. They seemed like real nice, regular kids to me then. Most were seventeen, eighteen, nineteen, maybe there was one guy who could have been thirty. Together, their pride made them speak up. Alone, they were just kids."

Paul Thai remembers his teenage years in the border camps from 1979 to 1981. "Boredom, crime, death . . . but we had the hope of America. It was in our dream, so it was better for us, but it was so hard to really believe that we'd ever get there. Then or now, it doesn't matter . . . a day in a refugee camp is a thousand years long.

"During the day, I sat and watched American people. Watched them in the light. Then I would think about what might happen, what would happen at night. In the dark. See, every day, every morning, when I woke up, I saw dead bodies. Or injured people. Or Thai soldiers searching for people. And we would hear rumors that the Khmer Rouge were coming to get us. Or the Vietnamese. Every day we felt like we would die that night."

The camps had no real work for their residents. Water was trucked in daily. Food was delivered. Refugees waited. For nourishment and drink and nightfall and sunrise. Paul says that the only alternative to waiting was writing. "I didn't speak any English, so I couldn't actually write any letters, but my older brothers went around getting help with letters . . . the writing of them, the sending of them. We wrote to everyone, every agency we heard of trying to get a sponsor who would help us get to America.

"When we saw Americans, we followed them and pulled on their pants, their skirts. We would grab hold and say, please take me with you, please don't let them kill me, help me.

"One time, in the camp, I saw a Cambodian who had sneaked in without being shot get caught by the Thai soldiers on duty in the camp. They put him in a jail and started beating him up. An American went up to the soldier and talked to him, spoke Thai to him, and the soldiers released the Cambodian. We all cheered. But then they took the American and put him in the jail and started beating him. There were hundreds of us watching and we began crying. We were glad that the Cambodian had been released, but we didn't want to see the American getting beaten. Americans were our friends. And this showed us that the American people were saving us all the time."

Americans and European volunteers were limited to extending their friendship only in the daytime hours. At sundown, buses arrived to take all non-Asians away from the border, back into Thailand where they stayed at night. According to Paul, "That's when we began shivering.

"The Khmer Rouge were still coming into the camp at night, trying to kill us. I was about sixteen years old then, and so I was old enough to help stand watch. We had a bell that we rang when we saw anyone that didn't belong there. One night I sat on my side of the camp with a friend and from the other side we heard a bell ringing, so I rang our bell. Then we saw Khmer Rouge running away. They knew if we all woke up and went after them, we could get them. We followed in the direction that we saw them running and we found that a couple of women had been raped and a couple of men had been killed. Anyway, that is what nights were like. We prayed that we would not be killed, that we would make it through the night. Until morning when the Americans came back."

Americans were cast in the role of savior again and again. Despite the fact that the Vietnamese were the ones who liberated the non-Communist Cambodians from the Khmer Rouge, American faces were the ones in which the light of freedom shone. And despite any analysis of American government policy that might show they played a role in paving or at least easing the way for the Khmer Rouge takeover in the first place, the majority of Cambodians still maintain that the Americans were their saviors.

They would not . . . did not . . . do not trust the Vietnamese. The centuries of hate and suspicion between Vietnam and Cambodia were not . . . are not . . . easily erased. A famous legend is told and retold by Cambodians of the Vietnamese invaders who long ago captured innocent Cambodians and buried them alive, vertically, up to their necks, then built a fire on the ground in the middle of them, using the heads of the Cambodians for cooking stones, to hold their kettle. This legend of the cooking stones is a story that will not easily go away.

"There is another story that the people tell again and again, too," says Paul. "It is like a prophecy . . . in Cambodian, it's a play on words. *If you go into the water, the crocodile is waiting for you. If you go into the jungle, the tiger is waiting for you. If you go into the forest, the thorn is waiting for you. If you go into the city, the police are waiting for you.* It just means that the Khmer people don't have any choices. The prophecy has said that there is no future for Cambodia, that one day our country will all be a part of Vietnam."

For the Cambodians who had survived Pol Pot time and who had endured the abuses that came with their escape to the border, Americans meant hope and freedom. And for many refugees, spending long tedious days in the camps, Americans also meant religious conversion.

"After more than a year in Khao I Dang, we were transferred to Mairut Camp. Food was better and we were further into Thailand, so that was good. It meant that we were getting closer to our dream. But there was still nothing to do. Nothing but sit and wait for your name to be called to go to America. There was an American missionary who was helping us. Even though we didn't speak English, we could understand because he had a Cambodian pastor with him who translated and taught us. My friends and I went to the church and listened to the pastor. The American and the Cambodian pastors taught us the Bible and tried to teach us about the American way of life because they knew we would be going to America. That is why I enjoyed it so much. It was teaching about the world, not just teaching about the church."

Paul had been a student at the monk's school in Poipet when the Khmer Rouge marched in and evacuated the city. The monks not only educated the boys in the ways of Buddha, but taught them academic subjects, languages, social customs, culture, and the ways of the world. "The monks were the educated ones, the good-hearted people, and the wise ones," says Paul. For the refugees, the American missionaries filled many of their deep and varied needs. The monks were gone, the temples and schools gone. As Paul and his fellow survivors prepared themselves for a new life, it seemed natural to follow this new path, one that led to Western religion.

"I was baptized while I was at the camp. I think it meant a lot to us that with American Christianity there was a one-on-one relationship. There was an American pastor who cared about us. As individuals. And who taught us," says Paul.

It is difficult enough to decide upon a curriculum for teaching American children how to read the English language in an American city, but what does a crew of various Americans—religious and secular, who keep irregular hours in a makeshift settlement where hunger, thirst, fear, and survival are the main obstacles, and where there is no common language let alone common cultural ground—decide to tell refugees about America?

Paul remembers one lesson. "They told us, when we walk on the streets in America, don't litter. Seemed like common sense to me. I couldn't remember that we threw trash on the street in Cambodia either.

"Also, they showed us a film that I remember so well. There was a Cambodian family, already in America, and it showed them shopping in a big grocery store. So much food! We couldn't believe it! The family in the film looked amazed, going around buying this and that with their sponsor. The film showed a car, explained that in America, people didn't walk or go around on their bicycle like in Cambodia, but instead people drove cars.

"The movie showed an airplane and the toilet in the airplane and explained how to use it. It showed the flight attendants serving the people. But I remember especially seeing the grocery store and thinking about having enough food to eat, because we were still hungry in the camps. Always hungry. And I remember thinking, oh boy, I'm going to have enough food to eat in America! And one day, I'll be in that car! And one day, I'll be on that plane!"

The pastor also warned them that there would be appliances such as dishwashers in America and that these conveniences might make them all lazy and unwilling to work hard and do things by hand. "I said I don't mind," laughs Paul, "I don't mind being lazy!"

When Paul's father's name, Kruy Chho, was finally posted, Paul ran to tell his family. "We knew this time was not like before, because this was Mairut Camp where we saw many Americans who cared about us. So we were sure we were not being tricked again. We knew we were going to America."

The journey to America began with a stay at the Transit Center Camp. Paul remembers that they knew they were getting closer to America because there was more food, better meals there. "We stayed two to three months there, then our names were called again. Then we went to Lumpini, and we were there three days before we got on the plane.

"From the very first time our name came up at Khao I Dang to move to Mairut Camp, we were ready. They kept giving us time to pack and prepare, but we were always ready, ready at Mairut Camp, ready at Transit Center, always prepared to leave, and prepared at Lumpini.

"Finally, when I saw the plane, I knew we were going to go, really knew we were leaving. At first, the plane seemed a little scary. We had never lived in a world where there was advanced technology. I had never really seen a plane. What happens if it runs out of fuel? If a car runs out, you can park it on the street, but what do they do with an airplane? What if it crashes, what happens, what do people do? What can people do? But we were happy to get on that plane because that plane meant getting out of Cambodia. It meant coming to America. It meant coming to the most powerful country. It meant coming to the world of technology. It meant coming to the land of opportunity. It meant freedom and education. Getting on that plane meant that there would be no more war. No more war for us."

Nine men were arrested on suspicion of robbery. And, in the apartment, $16,000 worth of stolen goods was recovered as well as weapons and rounds of ammunition believed to be meant for a machine gun. Ron Cowart was quoted in the *Dallas Morning News* the next day as saying, "We think there was some kind of meeting going on this morning. I don't want to say that we've broken their back, but we've made a big dent in this particular ring. . . . What we've done is shook them up."

Paul remembers that this bust was the big topic of conversation around the storefront for a long time. "Thao and I, especially, talked about this all the time. We talked and talked and talked about every minute of that morning. Then we went to the Cambodian family that was robbed and told them that we had recovered some stolen property and asked them if they would come down and check if it belonged to them.

"They came with us and when they saw their stereo and their watch and the rest of the things, they got so excited! They were saying, 'Look at the dent, look at the dent!' " After they picked out their property, they had to take a more difficult step. "We asked them then," Paul said, "if they would look at a lineup and try to identify the robbers.

"We had fourteen or fifteen people that included the guys we had arrested and we mixed them all up. First the husband came in alone and he picked out five men and said that those were the guys who had done it. He had no problem doing it, no hesitation. Then the wife came in and she picked out five with no trouble. 'This one, this one, this one, this one, this one,' she said, just like that—one, two, three, four, five. And they were all exactly the same guys that her husband had picked out before her.

"We had told the couple that they would have to go to court and testify against these men who had robbed them. We told them that it would be a long process. But the most important thing that we told them was that we would be with them. We would go to court with them, we would stand behind them—all the time, all the way through. That was the whole purpose of the storefront—so we could be involved all the way through!

"The trial took about two weeks. Every morning we called their bosses for them to explain why they had to be late that day or why they wouldn't be there at all. We drove them to court and translated everything for them. We waited with them in the room where they waited until it was time for them to testify.

"We couldn't do the actual translating in court for them because the defense attorney protested that—after all, we were with the police department, we were on the other side. But it was funny, because we knew the people who were doing the translating and sometimes there were things that they couldn't manage and they would look at us, and we would look at the attorney and he would look around. No one knew if we should be allowed to talk!"

The Vietnamese gang members were convicted and sentenced. After the trial, Little Asia residents began coming forward. Paul knows why. "They came in and started reporting crimes to us, started reporting suspicious things. They weren't so afraid anymore.

"It was because of two things. The first was because of what we told them about the gang members who had done the robbing. They had talked so tough and threatened the refugees so much that the victims didn't even think of the robbers as humans. We told them, 'Hey, they are just like us. Just people, just human beings. They even cried when they were caught.' " Paul adds, "At least when they were alone they cried. And the Asian people needed to know that, needed to know that they were just dealing with people—bad people, maybe, wild looking with scary-looking hairstyles, but not people who had superhuman powers to hurt them.

"The second thing the people needed to know was that we, at the storefront, would follow through. We had promised to be with the family who testified and we were. That was most important to the community—that we keep our promise to be there."

The storefront squad knew that they needed the trust of the refugee community in order to be effective. Asians victimized by Asians would be lost amid other priorities if the crime victims would not come forward and make themselves heard within the system. Without a partnership between the storefront and the Little Asia community, the gangs, the vandals, the dealers, and the robbers would never be caught. They would do their damage, again and again, only to disappear when pursued . . . swallowed up in a sea of Asian faces, eyes downcast.

7

A New American

We were running from the Thai solders. They were shooting at us and we were running for our lives. An old man had fallen and he reached up to me, asking me to help him. I didn't want to help him, I wanted to keep on running, but I stopped and tried to pick him up. I struggled and struggled with him, then I realized he was dead. He still reaches up to me, begging me to help.

—Paul Thai, describing his nightmares

A hard knock on an apartment door. A rush of adrenaline. Shouts. Obscenities. Bad guys jump from windows. Police draw guns. Good guys shout, "Police!" and aim guns. Bad guys shout, "Police!" and swear. Search. Handcuff. Threats from spike-haired Asian punks. Close-up on uniformed Asians. Satisfaction. Victory.

Again and again, Paul Thai and Thao Dam had replayed the scene. The bust. The trial. The conviction of the New Wave gang. Paul always concentrated on one detail.

"I kept remembering and thinking about the moment when Ron drew his gun. Two of the gang members came out of that window and acted like they were going to jump down on to the roof then somehow jump down into the alley and escape. I kept seeing Ron draw his gun. I would hear him call out for them to stop, to lay down flat—I would hear him call out that we were the police. And, in my mind, when I saw him draw his gun, I saw me draw my baton!" Paul laughs, "We were Asian PSOs, not cops. There is a big difference between holding a gun and holding a stick!"

When Paul, Leck, and Thao went through the Dallas Police Academy, firearms training was the only class they did not attend. Police service officers are authorized to carry batons only. No guns.

"I understand that rule," says Paul. "Most police service officers do the kind of work that frees regular police officers for more street work, more investigative work. PSOs might drive the vans that transport prisoners or they might work in the communities. They organize the bicycle rodeos at schools and talk about crime prevention to neighborhood groups.

"It's important work and I felt good about doing it. But I also kept thinking about that moment when Ronny drew his gun and I pulled out my stick. As someone who could give assistance to my partner, to Ronny in this case, I had felt useless. I don't remember feeling fear exactly, it was more of a feeling that I wasn't equipped to act—that I couldn't really help.

"That was the first time I started thinking about becoming a real cop. There were many considerations that went into the decision, but that was when the seed of that idea was first planted."

Another seed had been planted when Paul Thai's family landed at Dallas–Fort Worth Airport. From the moment the plane touched down, from the moment Paul entered the airport and saw the "hundreds and hundreds of American faces," he had wanted to become an American citizen. "We had repeated so often that America was the land of freedom and education, and I had believed in it for so long," remembers Paul, "that I can't remember when I *didn't* want to be an American citizen."

Certainly Paul could have lived a life of freedom in the United States and struggled for education and better living conditions as so many other Cambodians living in America do—without becoming a citizen—but Paul was on a steady course toward naturalization. Why? "Because then I would know for sure that I would never have to go back to Cambodia," says Paul.

There are Cambodian refugees in the United States who do want to return to Cambodia—when it is free—when the war, the wars are finished. They express a need to go back to find lost or missing family members, to see their villages, to be once again in the land of their ancestors, and finally, to be buried next to so many of their relatives who died in the killing fields so the family spirits, so brutally torn apart, can be reunited after death.

There are Cambodian refugees in the United States who simply find life in America too difficult, too confusing. They would return to Cambodia so they can once again feel that they are home. Yes, they know that their home would be a broken one, a land torn apart by war, still physically a mine field and a battleground, and still an emotional hell for those who remember and survived the holocaust. And yet, there are refugees with restless spirits that cannot find a resting place in America. Being lost in the language, the culture, and feeling unwelcome, different, poor, and without face, there are those who would go home and face the graveyard that was their Cambodia.

There are Cambodian refugees in the United States who would go home to fight. There are those who feel they can defeat the still-active Khmer Rouge. There are those who want to reclaim Cambodia from the Vietnamese-installed government. There are those who feel their homeland must once again belong to Cambodians, free Cambodians, and they are willing to go and fight that battle, both in the field and, if the promise of free elections is realized, at the ballot box.

Paul Thai shakes his head at the complexity of his countrymen and -women's feelings about their country. None of the emotions are simple. There is no joy at the freedoms offered in America that is left untempered by the loss of those who were left behind.

"When we first came to America in 1981," remembers Paul, "we were so happy. We talked to each other all the time about how wonderful everything was, how we were in heaven now, how we were born again now. And maybe we would be celebrating in some way, eating together or having a party with other Cambodians for New Year's or another celebration for another Cambodian holiday, and we would look at my mother and she would be crying. We would all be talking about how happy we were to be in America, and my mother was happy, too, but she would be sitting over in the corner of the room crying. None of us would say, 'Why are you crying, mother?' because all of us knew. My mother cried for our brother who was still in Cambodia. She cried for all of our family, all of our relatives whose bones were in the killing fields. She would be so happy for all of us. And she would be so sad for all of us."

Paul's father, too, feels the double-edged emotion of living in America. In their earliest days in Dallas, his oldest son, Mao, found a used cassette recorder for him to play. Mao taught his father how to insert the cassette tape and how to record his voice. Paul remembers his father, sitting in their small apartment, speaking into the tape recorder. Over and over, his father told the story of the Khmer Rouge invading the villages, driving Cambodians into labor camps, concentration camps, and into the killing fields. Again and again, Paul's father praised America for opening its arms to welcome the Cambodians. He grew more and more dramatic, louder and louder, chanting. After praising America, he would return to his subject—Cambodia—its history, its beauty, its horror, its peace, its war.

In 1986, when Paul was beginning to think about being a police officer, a full-fledged rookie cop—a step that held the prerequisite of at least forty-four college hours *and* U.S. citizenship, his family was beginning to feel a pull in another direction.

Customarily, Cambodian families remain together. Married children live with their parents and when a new generation comes along, grandparents delightedly help to care for them and exercise authority over their upbringing. Paul and Marina lived with Paul's mother and father, brothers and sister. By 1986, they had moved into a three-bedroom apartment that was fashioned from a two-bedroom apartment and an adjoining studio. A door had been put into the thin wall that had previously separated the two flats, and Paul's family happily filled up all the spaces. His parents had one bedroom for themselves, his brother Mao and his wife and three children had another bedroom, and Paul and Marina and their children had a third bedroom. Paul's unmarried brothers and his sister, Chandy, shared the living room area in a dormitory-style arrangement.

This kind of crowded living arrangement might cause an American-born American, raised on the promise of wide-open spaces or at the very least, a room of one's own, to shake his or her head in pity or concern over the lack of privacy for the individual families, not to mention the individuals them-selves. But in Paul's family's case, the concern is unfounded.

"We loved living this way. We liked being together, not being lonely. My mother and father helped look after the children so we all could work or study—there was always somebody to talk to or to help you with a problem. Sometimes, yes, it was crowded, and sometimes, yes, we would like more room for the children to play—and more yard for a garden. But most of the time, we were happy all together."

There were times, however, that some tension between Paul and the rest of the family surfaced. "My family often told me that I had a problem with saying no," says Paul, "and they were right. Many times I would get a call in the middle of the night from a Cambodian family that was having a problem and they would want me to come and help them. Actually, that still happens. I always went. I still go. Sometimes, I would be doing something with my own family, maybe planning to go to a friend's house, or just sitting down to have a meal, but if a call came in for me, I would leave to help. This made my family—some of my family—upset with me."

It wasn't the job with the Dallas Police Department that made Paul the first name on every Cambodian's lips when there was a problem. Paul had always been a visible presence in the community. He never refused to accompany a neighbor to the food stamp office, never refused to take someone to the doctor, the clinic, or the hospital. Paul never said no to a trip to the grocery store or, in the pre-storefront days, to the downtown police department for the fingerprinting necessary to get working papers and apply for aid and for citizenship.

Paul's pastor, Charles Morris, despite being one of his most frequent callers needing help with translation, often encouraged him to say no. "I was rapidly burning out myself—the needs in the community were so great—and I told Pov Thai that he should protect himself and learn to say no," remembers Morris.

"Yes, Chuck Morris told me to say no to people, but I couldn't," says Paul. "I wanted to help people, I wanted to be there when they called, but it was all for my benefit, too. My ESL teacher was always stressing that we should practice our speaking. I felt that I just couldn't turn down an opportunity to speak English."

Paul feels, too, that there were and are many other kinds of rewards involved in saying yes. "When I said I would take the pregnant women for their checkups at Parkland Hospital on Saturday mornings, I would think, oh no, a whole day waiting for seven women to see the doctor. But now, when I am on the street, there are a few kids who run up to me and talk to me, and finally one of them, asked, 'Don't you know me? I was inside my mother and you helped her go to the doctor.' The child's mother told him that he should pay respect to me because I was such a good friend to their family. This makes me feel so good.

"What if I had said no to Father Miltenberger when he asked me to transport the traditional dancers to their rehearsals and performances? If I had been too busy to say yes, I might not have met Marina.

"Marina is good about understanding most of the time, but she has a problem with me being gone so much," Paul says. "When Chet was born in 1984, I was still working at the printing shop and I took one day off. But when Maly was born on June 12, 1986, I didn't even take the day off. I had taken her to the hospital in the night and was there when Maly was born, then I left in the morning when it was time for work. I went to the hospital to see Marina during my lunch break and she told me to look over at another woman who had just had a baby and said that that woman's husband had been there the whole time and was with her the whole time afterwards. He had taken the whole day off from work, probably even more than one day! I said that I was sorry, but I had to leave and she said that I must love the community more than her if I only spend fifteen minutes with her when she is in the hospital!"

When asked if he knows the word "priorities," Paul laughs, "Oh yes, Marina and many people in my family are always telling me about my priorities—that I have them all wrong!"

Although some of his brothers told Paul that he should be taking better care of his family and spending less time and energy in the community, Paul's father supported his son's commitment. "My father has always been behind me in every way. He has supported me in my studying and my learning English and he supported me in the decision to take the job with the Dallas Police Department."

In the information booklet that Paul hands out to various civic groups in the Dallas area, "Understanding Cultural Differences," the differences between Americans and the Indochinese under the heading "Family Relationships" are delineated as follows:

AMERICAN:
- Family relationships are not always close.
- Usually, only two generations live at home.
- Older people may live in nursing homes or alone.
- Grown, unmarried children live separately and independently.
- The American family authority structure tends to be flexible.
- Spouses are considered equal, both legally and intellectually.
- Women are independent and have more legal and marital rights than Indochinese women.
- Family pressure is moderately effective at keeping its members in line.
- Divorce is no longer an unacceptable solution to marital problems.
- Children have a great deal of freedom and are supervised with only minimal corporal punishment.
- When guests visit, the children may or may not introduce themselves.
- Most Americans from all socioeconomic groups assign household tasks to their children as a methods of teaching them a sense of responsibility.

INDOCHINESE:

- Family relationship are very close, including the extended family.
- Often, three to five generations live in one home.
- Older people live with younger family members and never in nursing homes.
- Grown, unmarried children live at home with their parents.
- Indochinese family authority structure is very rigid. For example, the husband is the primary provider, and the wife's primary role is to take care of the home and children.
- The Indochinese woman is the master of the home and the finances. The man works to support the family and is the final decision maker in major family matters.
- Women are not as independent as their American counterparts and have fewer legal and marital rights. Socially, a divorced woman is an outcast. Close family cohesion places enormous pressure on the man not to divorce.
- Family pressure is very effective at keeping its members in line.
- Divorce is an unacceptable solution to marital problems.
- Children are under more strict control, and corporal punishment is acceptable.
- Children are expected to greet houseguests, be introduced, then be dismissed.
- Children in Indochinese families are assigned household tasks only if their family is poverty-stricken.

Paul's parents reflect many of the qualities that might be typed as *Cambodian,* but in many ways they are unusual. Although most Cambodian parents would encourage their children to be educated, they would be interested in education as a means to a job and a job as a means to financial security. The financial security of a Cambodian's children is also the financial security of the same Cambodian. As the mother and father get older, their grown children will provide for them. It is part of their cultural tradition that the parents and grandparents will be honored, respected and well cared for by the children.

Following this line of cultural reasoning, Paul's father should have encouraged him to stay at John A. Williams, Printer, where he was making a better salary churning out Pepsi advertisements than he was going to make risking his life in the uniform of the Dallas Police Department. Also, in keeping with

the traditional Cambodian way of thinking, Paul's father should have discouraged him from making the kind of waves that, as Police Service Officer
Thai, he would be required to make. But Paul speaks respectfully of his father,
proud that his parent has a more distinctive attitude.

"My father always wanted me to get the education that I wanted. When the
police department job came along, he saw it as a career, not just a job, and
I think he saw it as an opportunity to not only help my own community, but
also to learn more about being an American," says Paul.

Paul's father, through Paul as translator, says, "America opened its arms to
us. It is important to give back to America." No matter how innocent the
questioning or the questioner, Paul's father answers every query by saying
how much he loves America, how grateful he is to be in America. He offers
no opinion that might be somehow construed as a criticism. Although there
are several Cambodian groups in the United States who are considering the
possibility of returning to their country if elections are held, Paul's father says
he would not leave. He would like, perhaps, to visit Cambodia once again, to
look for his son, Muy, and to visit the temple at Angkor, but he emphasizes
that it would be a visit, not a return.

Paul says that his father always emphasized the family's good fortune in
getting to America. From the first night in the Welcome House Paul remembers his father constantly telling his children how wonderful America was to
receive them, that they should always be grateful.

"When we had been here a year or two, my brother Bun got discouraged.
He had a job somewhere and when it came time to do some layoffs, he got
laid off instead of an American who had come to work there after him. Bun
sometimes has a short temper and he came home and said he was 'pissed.' He
said that America was a dreamland when we first came here, but now people
look down on us, they take advantage of us. He said he didn't like America
anymore and he wanted to go back to Cambodia!

"My father got so mad! He told Bun never to talk like that, never to say
anything against America. He said that if Bun ever did anything against
America the whole family might have to go back to Cambodia and Bun would
be to blame. He asked him if he wanted to go back and suffer like his brother,
Muy, or if he wanted to go back to the killing fields," remembers Paul, "and
my father told him never to talk like that again, never to let anyone hear him
talking against America—America who opened its arms to us!"

In the 1800s, when Americans heard about the wide-open spaces and the gold "in them thar hills," thousands packed up their families and moved westward. Similarly, the promise of better jobs, more educational opportunities and more accessible government assistance has drawn thousands of Cambodians who had been settled elsewhere by various immigration agencies to California. Paul remembers hearing from friends he had known in the refugee camp who had been relocated to California. "They always said that we should come there because then I could go to school and our family could get better financial assistance. There were so many more translators, more helpful people in the government. But," says Paul, "my father always said, 'no.' He told us that he didn't want us to depend on government assistance anyway, that he didn't want to go where it would be easy to take money without working. He said that in Dallas we had jobs so we should stay in Texas.

"But things got more difficult. Bun had his problems with being laid off, and my oldest brother, Mao, experienced prejudice, too. Although," Paul laughs, "he didn't always know it was prejudice at first!

"Mao worked at a furniture factory here in Dallas for eight years, but in the first year he was there—in fact, right after the whole family came over here and joined him, a few days after the television he had bought for us was stolen—he came over to see us and asked me if I knew the American word *gotdam*? I told him no and said that it sounded like a Chinese word to me. He said no, that Americans used the word all the time. Then he asked me, how about *gotdam pepo*? He said people said that all the time to him, they would call him a *gotdam pepo*. I said I was sure that it was Chinese and we asked my mother since she spoke some Chinese dialects, but she said she hadn't heard of that—it wasn't any Chinese that she knew.

"Later we found out that it was 'goddamn people' that Mao kept hearing. His boss kept referring to him as 'one of those goddamn people' or said things like 'you goddamn people' when he was telling him how to do his work. Mao felt so bad that he was called names that he couldn't even understand. "But now," Paul says with a smile, "he is in college in California. Not knowing, not understanding people who were insulting him made him so sad, but it also made him want to learn the language and study more. He tells me that he is like me now, people calling him all the time to help translate!"

How did any members of the Thai family begin the emigration to California when the head of the household had spoken against leaving Texas?

"My brother Bun had met his wife when she was visiting friends in Dallas on a vacation," says Paul. "She lived with her family in Modesto, California. They fell in love, so Bun visited her there and asked permission to marry, and she moved to Dallas. When a distant cousin of hers came to visit her after she and Bun were married, the cousin and my brother Tang fell in love. So Tang went to visit her in Modesto and they decided to marry and Tang stayed in California. He wrote to my parents and said they should all come to California, that life would be much better, that educational opportunities would be much better."

Paul's father was not in good health when they arrived in the United States in 1981. Extremely high blood pressure, in addition to some limitations imposed by a stroke, prevented him from working outside the home. Paul's mother found a job in a Dallas laundry, but the intense heat and difficult manual labor involved exacerbated the migraine headaches she had suffered most of her life. In 1987, after nearly six years in Dallas, Texas, America, Paul's father overcame his worries about California making life too easy for his children. When his son, Tang, encouraged the family to move West, Paul's father agreed. "There were too many financial difficulties for them here in Dallas," says Paul, "and my parents thought it would be good to have more educational opportunities for my sister, Chandy, and my youngest brother, Many."

Paul's father, as head of the family, might have demanded or, at the very least, encouraged Paul and his family to move with them to Modesto, but did not. He told Paul instead that he should continue his work with the Dallas Police Department. "Two of my younger brothers, Chi and Pheap, were married and had jobs and they were staying in Dallas. My father told me that my work as a PSO was more than a job. He said it was a career and it would lead to more education and it would give me an opportunity to help my people. He wanted me to stay in Dallas. He also said that he thought they would come back someday, after they were better off financially.

"The funny thing about this was that I had been the one who had wanted to go to California ever since I had heard about it when we were at Khao I Dang. People at the camp had hoped to be sent there, mostly because they heard that California had good weather and heard rumors that it was a nice place and that there were a lot of Asian people there already. Also, since we had been in the United States, I had heard from other friends who lived in

California that they had gone right to school—not as a janitor like me, but as students—and now they were in college already!"

Paul had already told his father that he hoped to eventually be a regular police officer and his father understood that before it could happen, Paul would have to become a citizen. "He wanted me to continue on this path, to be a citizen, to get more education and to work hard and be successful in my career."

In early spring 1987, Paul's parents, his brother Mao and his wife and children, and his brother Many and sister, Chandy, left to join Tang Thai and his wife in Modesto, California. Brother Bun was going to follow them in a few weeks. "We had a big party the night before they left. We had a lot of food—I remember we ate a lot and talked a lot. We were all very sad at being separated, but no one cried then—except my mother—she always cried at parties. We knew that we were going to see each other again, but still we knew it wasn't going to be the same. Then, the next day, they left.

"That first night when they were gone, Marina and Chet and Maly and I were lost! We were in a three-bedroom apartment all alone for the first time. We went into the studio apartment that was connected to the original two-bedroom apartment and we closed the door to make the space smaller. Marina and I both cried because we were lonely. We took the kids into bed with us and slept like that, all of us together."

Paul, alone with his wife for the first time since their one-night hotel stay after their wedding, says after the first night, the first weeks continued to be very difficult for them. "The apartment seemed so big, and at night we heard so many noises. In that building, we knew it was probably rats that we heard, but to us, in the night, it sounded like ghosts."

Paul had no time to feel lonely during working hours as his schedule grew busier and busier. He went to classes at El Centro College every morning, working hard for both the credit—the college hours he would need when he filled out the application for the police academy—and for the citizenship exam he was preparing to take. After school he went directly to the storefront, changed into his uniform and became PSO Thai. After his shift was finished, he coached one of the soccer teams or the baseball team. To this day, though, he has never had time to learn the rules of baseball. "Shouting run, run, run works sometimes, though!" says Paul.

After coaching a sports team or helping some kids with their homework,

Paul often had to go directly to a meeting of the Cambodian Association which he served as vice president. Occasionally there was a meeting or a social function sponsored by the Cambodian Lions Club which Paul had started with the help of Ron Cowart. Luckily, this usually did not conflict with his girl scout troop's meetings. Troop 410, made up of mostly Cambodian girls, met on Sundays. On weeknights, after all of his "extracurricular" activities, Paul could return home to study—and if no one called him for an emergency run to the hospital or an urgent translation connected with a police matter, he might be able to get in a full night's studying before tiptoeing into bed, being careful not to waken Marina, Chet, and Maly, already snoring softly in the bed.

Following this routine had its disadvantages—fatigue, missed time with his family, and no time or energy for any kind of personal pursuits or recreation. But one advantage of Paul's schedule was essential—this kind of all-involving community work and educational pursuit left him so tired at night that he finally stopped hearing the ghosts—at least most nights.

"I have a few bad dreams still," says Paul. "I don't have them as often, but every now and then, I still wake up sweating.

"One time when we were running across a field, another killing field, one more time that the Thai soldiers were shooting at us, I tripped and fell down. A soldier was on top of me, standing over me so fast, and he had his bayonet pointed right at me, touching me. I closed my eyes and thought, I am dead now, then opened my eyes and the soldier was staring at me. Then he just moved his gun and backed away a step. I couldn't believe this, but it was happening. He was letting me go. I got up and ran, thinking he was still going to shoot me, but he didn't. I have never figured out why he did not kill me. But in my nightmares, I see that soldier. I see him standing over me and I feel all the fear of that moment. One more moment when I was sure I was going to die."

When Paul first arrived, the Cambodian nightmares were so intense, he would wake up screaming and run out of the family apartment, right out onto Live Oak Avenue. His brothers had to go outside and get him. They brought him, sweating and shaking, back into the apartment. His mother and father had to calm him down and reassure him that he was in the United States of America. There was no Thai soldier poised to kill him.

"Then there is the other nightmare, the one that doesn't come from the past," says Paul. "It's the one I have about being in America, living here, being myself here, working and studying, and suddenly, I am back in Cambodia. I look around and I realize I am there and there are soldiers around and everywhere there is death, and I keep thinking in my dream, what am I doing back here in Cambodia? I keep asking myself, what did I do that was so bad that made them send me back to Cambodia?"

Paul knew there was no medicine, no cure for the Cambodian nightmares. Every refugee had them and if they were ever going to go away, it would take time. Maybe a lifetime.

But the other dream—the one in which Paul wakes to find himself back in Cambodia—that is a nightmare that Paul could actively fight in his waking world.

Thai Sophal, known to his family and his entire community by his nickname, Pov Thai, became the naturalized Paul Thai on June 26, 1987. Phal, his Cambodian name, was pronounced the same as the American name, Paul, so the change in name did not seem so marked.

But the change that is involved with becoming an American citizen is dramatic. Paul, who like most Cambodians does not show a great deal of public emotion, was overjoyed as he left the courthouse on Commerce Street in Dallas. An American friend who attended a party Paul and Marina gave to celebrate the occasion asked in a cynical fashion why Paul was so excited about being an American. "Go to Cambodia for one day, just one day, and you will see why I am so happy," Paul answered him.

For an average, middle-class, American-born American with a history not ravaged by genocide, poverty, or starvation, one of the most common nightmares is the one in which the dreamer is forced into a situation and doesn't know what to do. For example, one might find oneself acting in a play, on the stage in front of an audience, and he or she doesn't know any of the lines, has no idea what the play is. Another variation of this dream is finding oneself taking a test, an important exam, and looking down at the paper, finding that he has never heard of any of the questions, let alone the answers—or that the test is printed in another totally undecipherable language.

Creating the perfect nightmare for the average American dreamer might be as simple as requiring everyone to take the United States Citizenship Exam.

Even for someone ordinarily undaunted by tests and not prone to nightmares, picking up a book such as a Barron's *How to Prepare for the U.S. Citizenship Test* is a sure method of inducing anxiety. At a certain time in most American students' lives they knew that there were seven articles in the

Constitution and could probably enumerate and explain the ammendments that make up the Bill of Rights. They might have even known during whose administration the Teapot Dome scandal took place and why and when the WPA was formed. But would even the most industrious student of American history and government know that the Virgin Islands were purchased from Denmark in 1917? Or could anyone, off the cuff, give a brief summation of Clay's Compromise Tariff of 1833?

Certainly these questions would not be asked on the citizenship test. But in the Appendix to the study guide there is a detailed time line that would defeat the heartiest American-born American. Imagine struggling through the language and feeling that these dates and facts had to be memorized in order to become a citizen. According to Paul, many Cambodians do imagine the struggle and decide not to apply for U.S. citizenship.

"Many Cambodians just do not feel that their English is good enough to be a citizen. Even if they learn enough for the jobs or for simple communication, many times they are shy about speaking. My mother is learning English now, but when she speaks, she puts her hand up, covers her mouth as she talks," says Paul.

To be fair to the Barron's study guide, there is a unit entitled "What You Must Know." In the introduction to that forty-five-page section, it is made clear that the most important requirements for citizenship are a knowledge of the English language, demonstrated by reading, writing, and speaking and a knowledge and understanding of the history, principles, and form of the United States government. At the end of the unit, there is a sample test with twenty questions. Those questions include ones about the meaning of the colors of the flag, the names and functions of the three branches of government and the Emancipation Proclamation. There is no question about the Clay Compromise Tariff!

However, the extensive appendix which includes a timetable of history following a section on U.S. presidents and accomplishments during their terms, is certainly a formidable chunk of information. If someone were led to believe that he or she might be tested on these pages filled with the dates and facts that provide an extensive overview of American history, it would likely produce anxiety in all except those who consider American history their field of expertise. Since there are 186 pages in the entire guide, with only forty-five of them in the section on what an applicant *must* know, it is not farfetched to imagine that many who are struggling with English as their second language *are* led to believe that this information, because it appears in this book, is vital and must be learned.

Because most Southeast Asians who had any educational opportunities in their own countries before coming to the United States are from school systems that required learning by memorization, these tables of information provide an insurmountable challenge for most. Paul says that most Asians whom he has tried to encourage to become citizens have been too shy about their ability in English, but also are certain they could not learn all that is required of them.

"I was lucky," says Paul. "I had the encouragement of everyone at the storefront—all my American friends and," Paul says, after looking over a variety of comprehensive citizenship exam study guides borrowed from a public library, "fortunately, I had a very small booklet to study from."

Paul had planned to time his citizenship exam to roughly coincide with the time when he would have enough college hours to apply to the police department for admission to the police academy. Thao Dam was also applying to take the citizenship exam and they were studying together for it.

By this time, spring of 1987, there were other regular police officers at the East Dallas Storefront besides Corporal Ron Cowart. Sargeant Jim Parker oversaw the operation and Corporal Lynn Dorsey also manned a desk on Peak Street. Dorsey, part of a narcotics task force, was less interested in the social service aspect of the storefront and more interested in the potential drug busting that could be done in the crime-infested neighborhood. He was also a big supporter of Paul and Thao's bid for citizenship.

"Dorsey and his partner, Michael Carew, knew someone at immigration, I guess," remembers Paul, "and our applications were processed very quickly. We were scheduled to take the test in June instead of months later.

"I was in summer school then. When I had first started taking classes for the GED, I went to El Centro College in downtown Dallas. After I got my GED, I started taking classes there toward my associate degree. At first I did it one class at a time—it was so hard to study the subject and still be learning the language at the same time—but by June of 1987, I was taking on more class work. In Summer Session I, I took three classes and in Summer Session II, I was signed up for two classes, so I was carrying fifteen hours that term. When I found out I would be taking the citizenship exam then, I had to really increase my studying. I was working at the storefront until 10 P.M. every night, too.

"Marina knew from the beginning, before we got married, that I wanted an education and that I wanted to keep going to school. I felt she was behind me 100 percent. She would say, go ahead and do what you have to do—I will take care of the house and the kids. There were times, though, that Marina would remind me that I had a wife and family, and she would want me to spend time at home. She would say she supported me, but she would also ask, isn't taking four classes considered full-time? Well, then, how come you push yourself and take five classes?"

Paul's answer to Marina's question or to anyone else who asks him about his commitment to work and education is usually a modest shrug and a simple, "I want to be educated. I want to help my people." Most Asians who are doing the same kind of neighborhood work that Paul is doing give similar direct answers. They rarely mention drive, career advancement, or personal fulfillment.

Thao Dam, Paul's fellow PSO at the storefront, describes his own background modestly. He studied agriculture at college, but during wartime, he worked resettling those displaced by battles and bombings. When a village was evacuated, overrun, or blown apart, Thao Dam helped families who were desperately trying to stay one step ahead of the land mines. After Saigon fell and the Communists took over, Thao Dam was put in a concentration camp for several years. He escaped with one of his sons and, as two of the "Boat People," they made it to a refugee camp and found United States sponsorship.

"My first job," he remembers, "was as a janitor at the San Antonio Zoo. It was a terribly degrading job. I worked picking up the candy wrappers and the pieces of litter around the zoo, then one day they offered me a promotion. I would make more money if I cleaned up the monkey island. I would be the janitor for the monkeys. I think, then, that I felt a little stirring of ambition, a feeling that I didn't want to do this job anymore."

Thao Dam uses the word ambition cautiously and explains that he means that he felt he could be doing something better with his life. Paul, listening to the conversation, agrees that he felt the same way when he worked as the school janitor.

"When we talk about ambition, it is not exactly the same as when American-born Americans have ambitions," says Paul. "We would be too shy to have ambitions that were very great."

"And," adds Thao Dam, "a difference between the Asian ambition and the

American ambition involves nature. Americans are always competing with nature, trying to tame it or improve it. You know, they want to build tall buildings, taller than the mountains, taller than everything natural around them. Asians feel more like they want to be in harmony with nature, at peace with everything that surrounds them."

"In fact," says Paul, "I can tell you how shy we felt about ambitions. I have said many times what a great honor it is to be a teacher in Cambodia, how being a teacher gives one's entire family honor. It is such a revered occupation, that to even *say* that you wanted to be a teacher would be considered as bragging—to even think about the possibility of it all.

"But I couldn't make this dream of being a teacher go away. In the Buddhist tradition there is a time where you bring an offering to the monks so they will pray with you for what you wish to happen. They dig a big hole and you bring things connected with your wish and throw them in so that the monks can help you. A lot of people want to be rich so they bring money and throw it in as an offering.

"When we were in the Khao I Dang camp, everyone brought their things to the monks as offerings and I got some money from my mother and I bought a little notebook and a pen with red ink. Those two things are the symbol of a teacher. So I took them to the monks and threw them in. I took the risk that people would laugh at me and ask who I thought I was, thinking I could be a teacher. But I wanted it so bad. I had to try.

"When we got to America, it was still a risk to say I wanted an education. But I did say it and I did start school. Got my GED. I began thinking about being a Dallas police officer. I began thinking about going to college. I began dreaming of being an American citizen. These were all risky dreams—someone might ask me who I thought I was, trying to do these things. But I wanted them so bad."

Paul and Thao helped each other study for the citizenship test as each took care of daily business in the storefront. As one did the weekly session of refugee fingerprinting at the front counter, the other might be reciting the names of the U.S. Supreme Court justices. When the date finally arrived for them to appear for their test, Paul felt ready but nervous. He had faced many tests—physical, mental, and psychological—but passing this test, the U.S. citizenship exam, would give a shape and meaning to his life that he had dreamed of long before he had even arrived in the United States.

Paul Thai and Thao Dam both passed the test handily and, together, became American citizens on June 26, 1987.

"My impression of how it worked was that if you proved you understood English right away, and if you knew the answers to the judge's first few questions, you would not have a very long test," says Paul. "I was asked only six questions—what are the meanings of the colors in the American flag and a few others like that. Nothing too difficult."

Paul and Marina celebrated with their friends in Dallas and called their family in California. Paul's father was especially proud. Now he had a son who was an American as well as a Cambodian. He had a son who could help his family stay in America. He had a son who could help his fellow Cambodians make new lives for themselves in the United States. And most important, he had a son, born Thai Sophal, now known as Paul S. Thai, who could stop running from the Cambodian nightmare and pursue the American dream.

Paul and Leck go over some of the endless paperwork at the storefront. A computer that prints in Khmer, Vietnamese, and Laotian among other languages has been a tremendous help in servicing the community (Credit: Catherine Rooney).

Paul fingerprints Little Asia residents. Fingerprints are essential for all refugees as they move on to apply for assistance, work permits, and citizenship (Credit: Mack Brown).

Paul celebrates the holidays with neighborhood children and other volunteers from Texas and the North Pole.

Paul's baseball team, the Green Monsters. He admits that he doesn't understand much about the game, but says that shouting, "run, run," seems to work pretty well.

Paul and Marina dressed for the Lion's Club parade. Marina wears a traditional Cambodian costume.

Not the traditional Cambodian costume. . . . Paul, after graduating from the police academy, poses with the family . . . Marina, their son, Chetra, and daughter, Somaly (Credit: Barbara Boyd).

Paul is
congratulated on
his police
academy
graduation by
Dallas mayor
Annette Strauss.

Paul is presented
with an employee
award from the
Dallas police
department. The
celebrity presenter
is Steve Kanaly
former "Dallas"
star.

Paul addresses a group as the president of the first Cambodian Lion's Club.

Paul doing traditional Cambodian dancing on the Cambodian New Year, April 15, 1990 (Credit: Sharon Fiffer).

Paul Thai, college graduate. On May 10, 1990, Paul received his associates degree from El Centro College. He is now a student at the University of Texas at Dallas studying for his bachelor's degree (Credit: Barbara Boyd).

Paul, Marina, Chet, and Maly in front of the John F. Kennedy Memorial in downtown Dallas (Credit: Catherine Rooney).

Paul standing in the center of the East Dallas Storefront office. A few of the flags that represent the multicultural makeup of the neighborhood are shown in the background (Credit: Catherine Rooney).

Paul in uniform as a rookie cop, Dallas Police Department.

8

Police Academy II

Forget it, Jake. It's Chinatown.
—*Chinatown*, 1974 screenplay by Robert Towne

For most Americans, particularly television watchers and moviegoers under twenty-one, a return to the police academy probably connotes another sequel in the "Police Academy" chain. These are stories of zany recruits who, through the most basic and slapstick humor, manage to take up approximately 110 minutes on film and provide questionable entertainment to the viewer while providing unquestionable profits to the movie's investors.

Paul Thai shakes his head at any mention of either high or low comedy involved with his second time through the Dallas Police Academy. But he did experience the highs and lows of a dramatic exit from the storefront and an equally dramatic entrance into the academy.

"One more reason that I wanted to go the academy and be a regular cop was that it would open up a position at the storefront for another Cambodian," says Paul. That was one more job in a very narrow market and Paul was pleased that he could do his part in providing the opportunity.

"There were many people in the community who didn't want me to leave the storefront," remembers Paul, "I mean, besides Marina, who didn't want me to leave either! But Ron Cowart was behind me. He was very supportive.

"Even though, a few years before, I had not imagined myself as an American cop and had spent my time dreaming of being a teacher, I felt that this was, at least, going to take me in the direction of education. I had gotten forty-five college hours in order to get into the academy, and that was forty-five more hours than I thought I would ever have."

At Paul's farewell party, he admitted having some mixed feelings about leaving, but was excited about the possibilities outside of the Little Asia neighborhood. "One very important goal of mine was to be a role model," says Paul. "Little Asian kids, especially Cambodian kids, have very few role models. It becomes more and more difficult to convince a Cambodian kid not to drop out of school when he is being confused by all kinds of different attitudes from his family and from the American kids he is at school with.

"Asian families are telling their kids that they must go to school to learn, they must have discipline and respect for their teachers. But the kids go to school and on the way they see other kids with wild, punked-up hair and wild clothing, carrying big stereos and playing music. Do you think those kids are going to school to learn?

"So even though I know I am not so smart or so special, I felt that maybe if I continued studying and became a cop, I would show some kids that I am just like them, but I could do it. And if I could do it, they could do it, too."

Anyone who even occasionally picks up an American newspaper can read countless reports concerning the state of education in the United States—politicians' rhetoric that expresses concern for students and with the poor state of inner-city schools clashes daily with the features that report the lack of funding for the early childhood programs that have been proven links to later educational success. Magazine articles and books propose that parents become advocates for their children in the schools and become partners with the teachers—united in an effort to educate their children. Sadly, many teachers aren't encouraged by either salary or parental or administrative support to remain involved—figuratively and/or literally—in their once chosen field of teaching.

Paul Thai, aware of these mixed messages, is more concerned than critical. "I believe that people can do something about situations—in schools and communities—and so by going to the academy, I would be doing something positive about these situations."

American popular culture sends mixed messages about practically everything to its consumers. In the first half of the 1900s, a literary figure such as Thomas Wolfe might insist repeatedly in his work that you can never go home again, but a perky Debby Reynolds can turn sentiment inside out mid-century when she sings about love being lovelier the second time around. This clash of romantic themes—the latter advocating a return home, taking another chance, being unafraid of trying something again and the former insisting that nothing in life can be repeated, that nothing will have the charm, the depth, the truth, or the passion of the first time—is constantly repeated in literature, music, and film. And in the movies, this clash is not only explored thematically, as subject matter, but "going back" has become a part of the process of filmmaking.

The *sequel* is a curious American phenomenon. Although nonAmerican moviemakers have occasionally returned to familiar characters and settings in their work, it usually comes about when one director decides to further explore a character for artistic purposes. In American sequel-making the purpose is monetary. The oversimplified math is figured something like this— if one film about ghost busting makes money, two films about ghost busting will make twice as much money. If one film about silly recruits at the police academy makes money, won't five films that chronicle the slapstick adventures of police recruits make five times as much money? Therefore, it can be counted on that someone, somewhere, will repeat a financially successful movie formula until it ceases to be profitable.

Because of this nonwork non-ethic, most movie critics and movie fans complain about sequels. They insist that the "return" never holds quite the same substance or the same excitement as the original. The second film is often seen as a diminished, watered-down version of the first.

Life should not imitate the nonart of bad filmmaking, however, and in 1988, Paul Thai had every reason to expect to get more out of his second time through the Dallas Police Academy.

"I knew what to expect anyway," says Paul. "I knew how to do the exercises—the jumping jacks—and I had taken all the courses, taken all the exams before, so I wasn't nervous about the studying.

"Of course, I don't know how I did on the tests the first time through. For some reason—I guess they didn't take the PSOs as seriously as students in the academy—they never told us our grades. Thao, Leck, and I would take the test with everybody else, and they would give everybody a grade except us. They would just tell us that we passed. This time, I knew I would get to see my grades on everything."

So the metaphor of a movie sequel to describe Paul's second time around in the police academy ideally should have been too much of a stretch, too labored a set of thoughts for what really should have happened in 1988. Unfortunately, though, many of the criticisms that are most often applied to a movie sequel—character motivations going awry, confusion, conflicting purposes, and mixed and misguided intentions—apply as well to Paul's training as a rookie cop with the Dallas Police Department.

Paul's first encounter with an American policeman—watching through a crack in the doorway as an American officer shook hands with his bewildered father, promising to do his best to recover the family's stolen television—was an assuring one. His second personal encounter with an officer who stopped him for a missing taillight and issued him a ticket was a surprising one—the officer called him *Mister* Thai. But it was Paul's meeting with Ron Cowart that gave him his first, deeply felt impression of an American policeman.

Corporal Cowart, although he insists that police work—not social work—was and should always be the mission of the East Dallas storefront, defines police work, *community* police work, in somewhat different and broader terms than many of his fellow officers. Cowart's policing includes the long, slow process of educating a community, building trust, involving the police with the community as partners in crime prevention. It also includes going after the bad guys, but much of the daily work does revolve around feeding hungry people and helping find shelter and clothing for those in need.

Some of the officers who shook their heads as they found themselves handing out bags of rice over the counter at the Peak Street station often joked about being assigned to *Saint* Ronnie's storefront. The sarcasm intended by those police officers who used that title is ignored by Paul and other community members. When asked about Ron Cowart's sainthood, the refugees nod quite seriously. To the members of the Little Asia neighborhood, Ron Cowart is a saint.

Paul, although he firmly believed in Cowart's goodness and generosity, was aware that there were philosophical differences between Ron and some of the other officers stationed at the storefront, but those seemed like differences in priorities, in agendas. Most of the officers whom Paul worked with seemed, to him, to want to help the people in the community, even though there were those whose methods were quite different than Cowart's. And although Paul recognized that there were different kinds of cops, he saw Ron Cowart as his primary model.

"Ron Cowart was not only a saint to our people. He was a hero. To us, he represented the American police officer, not just a Dallas police officer. We would see television programs and see what the police did on those shows, but no one believed that was real—they were just stories. We believed that Ron was the model for all United States police officers. So that is what I wanted to be," says Paul, "a police officer like Ron."

Paul was not aware of any negative attitudes toward police from Americans. He remembers that occasionally he would meet people from his own country who had not met any officers like Ron Cowart and, consequently, did not have trusting or positive feelings toward the police. "Sometimes if someone doesn't know I work for the police department they will say that some ugly, unfriendly American policeman just gave them a ticket . . . or something like that," laughs Paul. "But I think that any Asian who could have his first experience with an American police officer like Ron would have positive feelings. The ones who met Ron first feel that the American police officer is trying to be fair and do a good job.

"Even if they do worry about the police, most Cambodians think that the American prisons are more than fair. One Cambodian man that I know, just a short time after he had gotten here to the United States, had gotten into a fight behind his apartment building and another man had pulled a knife on him and when he fought with the other guy, he ended up killing him. I think it was considered self-defense, but this guy still was convicted of something and had to go to prison for a short time.

"When he got out and I saw him he told me that it was wonderful! It was like a vacation to him. He described the three meals he had every day, and he said that he had a television to watch, and there were classes and sports and places to exercise. He thought it was wonderful!

"In Cambodia, a prison was never considered a place for rehabilitation. It was considered a place for punishment. Many times, it was considered a place for torture and death.

"For one of my criminal justice classes, we took a field trip to TDC, Texas Department of Corrections, and I remember that I understood what this guy had been talking about. It did seem like a vacation spot. They even had GED classes there."

Paul entered the police academy for the second time with an idealistic vision of American police, the Dallas Police Department, and the American justice system in general. To many of his fellow students at the academy he may have seemed naive. Paul, in spite of his doggedly optimistic view of the police at that time, does remember that he had heard that there might be a negative side to some members of the police department.

"There was a group of Laotians that came into the storefront who had their first police experience with patrolmen in another area of Dallas. They said that the police beat them up. At first I didn't believe them, but there were several who told the same story. They said that police talked tough to them and called them gooks and Vietnamese. One policeman said that his brother had been killed in Vietnam and so he didn't like to see any Vietnamese around Dallas. I guess the group of Laotians tried to say that they weren't Vietnamese, but their English wasn't that good. They got beat up. This happened in 1986 and it took me a long time to really believe what they were saying. It took me until I was on the street myself."

Before Paul went on the street himself with the Field Training Officers, he attended the academy. In April, 1988, Paul once again began the twenty-one weeks of training that, this time, would lead him to the ranks of rookie cop. An American-born American might say that the second time around would be simple, easy, maybe even a snap! But it would be against Paul's nature to express that kind of confidence openly. He simply says he felt no fear, but because of good memories of the first time through, he was excited about the prospect of once again attending the academy.

The first time, with Thao and Leck as his classmates and Ron Cowart as mentor and advisor, the academy was a wonderful experience for Paul. It combined the beloved school situation with training for a job that Paul believed was honorable and valuable to his own community. And although Marina disliked his taking a cut in pay to join the department as a PSO, her fears about her husband wearing a police uniform were more easily tamed since he was not going to become a real cop, or wear a gun. This time, knowing that Paul was in training to face the streets as an armed officer, Marina did not remain calm. Publicly she acted the part of the good Cambodian wife—quiet and supportive—but privately she was worried and upset with Paul. She stayed in close telephone contact with her mother who, like Paul's family, had moved to California with other relatives, and she began urging Paul to think about leaving for the West Coast. But Paul was unmoving. Expressing loyalty to his first American city, he insisted, "I am a Texan now," and equally loyal to his police role model, Ron Cowart, he was determined to follow in the footsteps of his mentor and become a Dallas cop.

In April of 1988, Paul Thai began academy life for the second time. He climbed the steps into the building and walked into the lecture hall. Since there were no familiar faces to spot—no Leck Keovilay, no Thao Dam motioning him over to a saved seat, he found a place and quickly sat down. Quietly and efficiently, he began taking notes, preparing to take the classes and the tests as seriously as he had the first time, knowing this time he would be graded, this time his scores would matter.

The most uncertain score would be the one he made at the gun range. Never having officially taken the firearms training, Paul was delighted to report that he scored a ninety-four. "I was happy about that because I was nervous holding the gun for the first time. I'm not ever nervous now, because I am used to it, but I can clearly remember picking up the gun and thinking to myself, uh-oh, what am I going to do now?"

Studying and scoring well on the tests were tasks that Paul could control and accomplish. Getting to know his fellow class members and establishing friendships was another matter. On the first day, there were two other Asians in the class. One dropped out after only a few days and the other, a Laotian, dropped out after failing a test in the second month of training.

"It was hard being the only Asian at the academy. Before, I could look around and find Leck and Thao and because we got to know each other, studied together, worked together, and learned to trust each other, we became like brothers," says Paul. "We are still like brothers even though our backgrounds are so different.

"This time through at the academy, I didn't make friends in the same way. I did meet some people and we were friendly, but it was not close. I would not call them my 'buddies.' Sometimes I felt that people didn't talk to me, didn't even see me, because of the way I look. But other times, I think maybe, it's because I can't talk about baseball or football.

"I don't mean to criticize, but I was so surprised to hear people talk for hours and hours and hours about football or baseball. I don't mean to be picky, but it just didn't quite interest me. And also, I just don't know anything about it. So it would go like this—someone would say hello to me, how are you and all that, and I would answer and think we would start to have a conversation, then someone else would come along—another American—and the person talking to me would turn to the new person to say hello and one of them would ask if we had heard what the Cowboys did or if we had seen the Rangers do this or that, and suddenly I wouldn't be in the conversation anymore."

Although there are those who might think Paul exaggerates the importance of sports knowledge in the art of American conversation, there is one enterprising Georgian, Barry Dreayer, who has based his business on the premise. His company, TeachMeSports, offers five-hour seminars that teach the basics of football. Soon he hopes to branch out into TeachMeSports videos. Dreayer says that only about twenty percent of his students in each class are men—signifying that men are either more confident in their knowledge of sports or are more reluctant to admit what they don't know—and that most of those twenty percent are not American-born American men but recent male immigrants.

"This is how it worked," says Paul. "I would be in, then another American would come along, and I would be out. That is something I noticed about Americans when they talk to Asians. They are interested, but when another American comes along, they just start talking to that American, and they leave the Asian out."

Paul found that, one-on-one, there were classmates who were intermittently interested in his background and his country. He found himself explaining several times that Cambodia was its own country, not a part of Vietnam, as many believed. He located it in Southeast Asia for curious classmates who had no idea where such a place was on the globe. There were a few classmates who had seen the movie *The Killing Fields* and Paul would begin to explain what it was like in Cambodia in 1975.

Like Haing Ngor, the actor who portrayed Dith Pran and who wrote his own story, *A Cambodian Odyssey,* Paul believed that the movie didn't portray half the horrors that really went on during Pol Pot time. "In the movie, I never saw people buried alive or families being torn apart while mothers and children screamed and cried and I didn't see people hung in the middle of a big meeting, then stabbed to death while everyone was made to watch. Those things I saw with my own eyes, but I didn't see them in the movie, so I would have to agree that the movie was good in what it showed, in what it tried to teach about what happened, but it was much, much worse to be there and see all that really went on," says Paul. "But the movie was a starting point that I could use to explain things to people . . . if they asked."

The people who did ask sometimes wanted Paul to tell them stories about what happened, but Paul found that few stories were finished. "I might be answering a question, then someone would come in and talk about Walker. About trading players. I would ask Walker who? Or who Walker? Trade for what? And they would ask me, 'You don't know who Herschel Walker is? How long have you been in the United States? How long have you been in Dallas? Don't you know anything? Don't you read the paper? Don't you follow the Dallas Cowboys?' So then I would be out of the conversation.

"I don't think anyone was trying to be real mean. It was just that the Dallas Cowboys aren't real important to me. I do read the paper. I read the news about Cambodia and what is happening there and in the refugee camps. I read the paper and try to improve my English and try to know all the important news that is happening in the country. I do want to talk about news that I read in the paper, but I don't have time to learn about the sports and read the sports pages. Not yet.

"It's funny, because Ronny had a Superbowl party in the first or second year we had the storefront and he invited Leck and Thao and me to his house to eat and watch the superbowl. I tried to understand the game, but I was lost. Thao Dam, too, but not Leck! He really understands football and he loves to watch it. I think that is because he has lived in the United States longer. And," Paul adds, "Leck came here as a student, not as a refugee. Maybe it's harder for refugees to learn football."

Paul is always respectful when he speaks about America and Americans. He is apologetic when he says, "I think Americans know many things about Vietnam because there is so much on television and so many books on that subject. Also because of the involvement in the war. But it seems like there is a lot of history and geography that Americans don't know. They don't know about Cambodia and about the Communist time.

"Many of the people who do know something about Cambodia don't know that the Khmer Rouge flag flew at the United Nations—as recently as 1990—and the Khmer Rouge had a seat there. It is amazing to me that this is true and when I tell people this, they are shocked.

"But, then again, there are so many things I don't know—like football and baseball," Paul says.

In spite of that woeful sports information gap, Paul scored well on all the tests administered at the academy and graduated from Class 206 of the Dallas Police Academy on Friday, September 2, 1988. An article in the *Dallas Morning News* was headlined, "Dallas Force gets first Cambodian police officer" and a picture of Paul Thai holding his diploma, looking seriously at the camera accompanied the feature.

After graduation from the academy, the newest Dallas police officers begin their field training. This is done, one-on-one, on patrol with a field training officer in four phases. There are three seven-week assignments, then one three-week assignment which totals twenty-four weeks of on-the-job training.

Monday, September 5, Paul Thai reported to the central division of the Dallas Police Department to receive his first street assignment.

Paul's first Field Training Officer—FTO, for short—was not waiting next to the patrol car when Paul got his orders on Monday. Paul's first assigned FTO was on vacation. So Paul rode with someone else, not his own FTO, and the substitute FTO told him just to sit back and watch him work. Paul was told to cover other officers in an emergency, but as far as the routine business of patrol and answering calls—they would handle it—he would learn by watching them.

The next day, Paul was told to ride with someone else. Again, he was told to sit back and watch. "This, I believe, is normal," says Paul, "that the rookie just sits back and watches the first week. I don't think any rookie is allowed to make any decisions or anything like that.

"The problem, though, was this. That first week of observing was when I was supposed to be learning the routine, learning how to handle myself and situations that would come up when we were out there on patrol. But my FTO, the officer who would judge me and give me my grade, was on vacation while I was doing this observing. And I was observing other officers, doing things their way.

"The second week, when I met my FTO, he was criticizing me from the beginning because of the way I did things and I told him that it was the way I observed things being done the previous week and he said to forget about that. He said, 'I am your FTO and you are supposed to do things my way!'

"I couldn't criticize back, but I did feel that if an officer is going to be an FTO, he probably shouldn't be on vacation the first week that training begins. That doesn't seem like the way to get things off to the right start.

"One of the things that was so confusing to me concerned the safety rules. We were always taught that when you approach any suspect, even if you think he is probably a nice guy, you must search him and make sure he doesn't have any weapons. That is not always easy because sometimes you know the person and you might want to start talking to him first, but the rule is to search first. You search everyone except the victim of a crime . . . well, actually, sometimes you search the victim, too! But anyway, you make them put their hands on their head and you go through the routine search. That is what I learned at the academy and it is what one of my first FTOs told me to always do.

"But when I got a new FTO, we responded to a complaint about someone loitering. I began to search the guy and the FTO came up and asked me what I was doing. I told him I was doing a routine search for weapons and he told me no, that I shouldn't do that because this guy was just an old wino. Harmless. I said, 'Wait a minute, I was taught safety first at the academy and from the other training officer,' and this FTO said to me, 'No, I am your FTO now.'

"Another time I got the FTO so mad at me! It was the first time I put the flashing light on and the siren and was driving and I approached an intersection where there were cars and people in the way and I slowed down a little, and my FTO started yelling at me. He was shouting, 'Why did you slow down, you already have your light on and your siren, you are never supposed to slow down' and on and on. So I said, 'I'm sorry, sir, I thought I should do this for safety.' I was taught about safety and he cut me off and said to me, 'You're in my world now!'

"The thing that I finally realized is that each FTO creates his own world. Every time I would mention the academy or that another FTO had told me to do something another way, the FTO I was with would scream that I was with him now. When I began to catch on that I had to do it every individual's way, I asked one of my trainers for a second chance. He said no and walked away."

Ron Cowart had taught Paul and the other PSOs at the East Dallas Storefront that one of the police officer's jobs was to build trust in the community. Following Ron's example, Paul usually approached people with a quiet, questioning manner, and characteristically for a Cambodian, he was polite. His field training officers, although some were more understanding than others, generally agreed that he needed to be more assertive. "Assertive" was the operative word, the word that appeared on reports, but to Paul's face they told him to be mean, to be tough and to talk loud.

"They told me I was too friendly and nice. One of them said because I was Cambodian I was too trusting. They told me to stop smiling at people—that I should never smile at anyone unless I was relaxing and not on duty.

"I understand their point, but I guess I thought that if I was approaching someone and was acting reasonable—not friendly, not vulnerable, but not yelling and shoving either—I thought I could get more information. It seemed to make sense to me that with some of the drug dealers, if you acted civil to them and acted like maybe you could be their friend, that they could trust you, they would give you the information you needed. If you yelled at them and shoved them and demanded their IDs, they wouldn't talk to you at all.

"My first seven weeks in the field were in downtown Dallas. There weren't really that many problems with that one. My score was okay. My second seven weeks was in an area a little farther east than East Dallas. That was okay, too. I made a perfect score on that phase. My FTO never had to do anything—he just watched me—he allowed me to make all the decisions.

"My third phase was when I was in trouble. That area was South Dallas where a lot of the drug dealers and gangs are. When there is a call for help in South Dallas, they always send three cars instead of one. I was assigned to the shift called 'deep night'—midnight until morning. From the beginning, my FTO down there was criticizing me, calling me an Oriental and saying I was too nice and too polite. He said I was going around bowing to everyone." Paul pauses and says steadily, "He was wrong. I don't bow to crooks."

9

Deep Night

"There was a man who owned a dog and a pig," said Paul's mother, rocking and patting the youngest, but gazing around at all of her children, stretched out on their sleeping mats in a circle under the whirring ceiling fan.

Every night, after closing, Paul and his brothers put the chairs on the tables, mopped the restaurant floor until it was spotless, then the family prepared for sleep. The floor was the coolest place to lay their heads.

"And the man said to the animals, 'In this country, you must work very hard—whether you are a human or an animal—in order to get food to eat. So whoever works the hardest will get the best food.' The man owned a rice field and he told them he would be able to tell who worked the hardest by looking in the field. Whoever was the best worker would leave the most footprints. The man said he would return the next day to check his field.

"The pig went out and worked so hard. He left footprints all over the rice field. He was tired after that and came home to rest.

"Early the next morning, while the pig was still sleeping, the dog ran out into the field. He didn't do any work, he just ran all around, brushing away the pig's footprints and leaving his own.

"When the farmer came and looked at his field, he saw the dog's footprints and thought he must have worked very hard, so gave dog a good meal. Then the farmer went home and ate the pig."

A traditional Cambodian folktale

Paul Thai, when he was still a boy, had survived on a few hours of sleep a night for years while working at backbreaking manual labor in the Khmer Rouge camps in Cambodia. When his family escaped to the refugee camps along the Thai border, they found that, in order to protect their meager belongings and more importantly, their lives, few people slept through the night. And although life kept improving for him after he came to the United States, Paul never managed to keep the kind of schedule that would allow him an eight-hour night, an eight-hour workday, and eight hours for family, friends, and himself. His jobs, his overtime, his studying, his family responsibilities, and his community work that kept him on call twenty-four hours a day never allowed him a full night's sleep.

So for Paul, the "deep night" shift did not present a problem because it would rob him of his rest. He required little and demanded less. He approached this phase of his training with no more apprehension than he did the other phases, but because of the assignment's location, he kept a healthy respect for the seriousness and the dangers of the duty.

Marina had grown used to being alone with the children. There were still friends in the building with whom she could spend time in the afternoons and evenings while their children played together in the dusty concrete courtyard that the building surrounded. There were television programs that she could watch, privately practicing her English pronunciation along with the characters on "General Hospital" or "All My Children." There was the telephone, her link to her mother who was now living in San Diego. But these avenues that led her out of isolation during the afternoons and evenings while Paul worked or studied were closed to her in the late hours of the night and early hours of the morning. For Marina, "deep night" became a time of fear and loneliness.

Paul and Marina had both been aware for a long time that the Little Asia neighborhood, despite its feelings of familiarity and comfort, was not a safe place to live. The Asians served by the storefront had learned to trust the police and report crime, but because so many of the young and healthy refugees, the ones who had made such excellent neighbors and friends, were learning better English and moving up to better jobs, they were moving out of the area in search of better housing and better schools for their children.

New neighbors were mostly Hispanic and black, also in search of low-income housing but not always tolerant of neighboring Asians who didn't speak English or understand American rules of the road. Paul, because of his police training and his work at the storefront, was aware of the growing number of crack houses and the buildings out of which both big-time and small-time drug dealers operated. Marina, because of her own observations of people coming and going in the neighborhood, knew that Little Asia, even in daylight, was never really a completely safe place and during deep night, alone with the children in the apartment, it was a completely scary place. She began to talk to Paul about it, asking him to reconsider his decision about being a police officer, begging him not to leave her alone at night.

Paul tried to reassure Marina. He reminded her that this field training was the last three-week session, then after three more weeks on a different shift, he would be a full-fledged cop. He told her again about the salary increases he could regularly expect as a real police officer. He told her that he could continue going to school, continue to advance in his career. And he reminded her that all of these advantages—the money, the important work, the education, and the status—would bring them closer to the kind of American life they wanted to lead, the kind of American life they wanted to hand down to their children. And to reassure himself as well, Paul said that he would be a role model for all Cambodians who came to America and were afraid to dream and were too shy to believe they could reach worthwhile goals. Then he would leave the house to go to work.

While riding around South Dallas on patrol during that shift, Paul had the feeling that he and his FTO were the only ones in the world who were awake. "It felt like it was just us and the bad guys out there every night," says Paul. But it wasn't the bad guys who changed Paul's mind about being a cop.

The first few nights Paul rode the "deep night" shift, his FTO declared himself *not* a "Ron Cowart" kind of cop. The beat in South Dallas was a far cry—more like a bloodcurdling scream—from the East Dallas storefront in Little Asia. Although the trainer asked a few questions about Paul's background, about his life in Cambodia, he responded quickly that it was clear to him that the Cambodians were too friendly. They allowed what happened to happen in their country. And his FTO also made it clear to Paul that Cambodians seemed to him to be far too friendly on the street to make it as cops.

"He told me that I asked too many questions. I was too polite. He said I should talk tough from the beginning. I should never smile. I should be mean. That was how I was supposed to act if I wanted to be a cop," says Paul. "He kept this up all the time."

Back in Little Asia, Lynn Dorsey, a corporal stationed at the storefront who worked with Paul and who helped him prepare for his citizenship exam and his return to the academy, says that the single most important quality for a cop is common sense. "I think Paul would make a good cop because he does have common sense," says Dorsey. "Not all Asians have it, not all Anglos have it, but Paul Thai definitely does."

Dorsey is quick to point out that although he and Ron Cowart worked together and have known and respected each other for several years, he himself isn't a "Ron Cowart" type of cop either. He didn't mind his storefront duty because it gave him a chance to chase and sometimes catch the drug dealers working the neighborhood, but he didn't like the social work involved or the social work label attached to working at "St. Ron's storefront."

Dorsey believes in helping the Asians out of the neighborhood, helping them advance toward bigger and better American dreams. In the old debate over whether a helping hand will soon become a handout, he represents the side that says to help the refugees, then move them up and out—give them the means to independence without allowing them to become dependent. Not as openly responsive to the question of cultural differences between Asians and Americans as Ron Cowart, Dorsey responds on an individual basis. "I don't know about Cambodians or any Asians in general, but Paul Thai would make a good cop. He just got the wrong FTO to work with. They had a personality clash. I already told the sergeant here at the storefront that I would gladly volunteer to be his FTO. I would love to be his trainer in the field, because I know he has what it takes."

Dorsey, who shrugs off the obvious affection he has for many of the community people coming in and out of the storefront, rolls his eyes upward when he is called away to drive a teenage Cambodian girl to a secondhand store to help her pick out a prom dress. "I don't know why she likes me so much, but I'm the only one she'll let take her," says Dorsey, shaking his head, but allowing himself a slight smile.

Ron Cowart also heard from Paul about what was happening in his training. Paul sat across the desk from Ron and tried to describe his nights riding in the patrol car. Suspected perpetrators were spitting on him, calling him a dog or Vietcong or worse, telling him that they had fought for his people in Vietnam, and now who did he think he was trying to arrest them? Being abused by the bad guys was all in a day's work for a cop, but he was also constantly harangued by his FTO, who criticized his manners, his bearing, his heritage, and his lack of "assertiveness"—the buzzword that kept being thrown at Paul.

Ron Cowart was in a quandary. He understood Paul's anguish and he understood what was happening because of the sterotyping by the FTO. He listened to Paul tell him about his training. Paul did not complain, did not accuse, but by his manner and in many of the things he could not say or chose not to say, he revealed to Ron that he felt himself to be in an impossible situation. Paul knew in his heart he could be a cop and yet was being told nightly, both in words and actions, that he would never make it.

Paul Thai had experienced and resisted some of the most relentless brainwashing ever practiced, survived hard labor under some of the most devastating working conditions, and had been starved and tormented under one of the cruelest regimes in history. That was Cambodia, "the land of death," as Paul describes his homeland.

This was America, the land of freedom and education, where Paul had struggled to learn the language, become a citizen and make a home and life for his family as well as bring honor to his own Asian community. Now Paul had to struggle with the fact that if he quit or if he didn't make it, after all the abuses he had survived to get to the United States, he would be caving in to old-fashioned, nonviolent American prejudice. Paul, however, doesn't allow himself to describe his treatment as prejudice. "I don't like to accuse people of prejudice, but maybe this was something like it—my trainer kept saying, 'you Asians do this,' or 'all of you Asians think that,'" says Paul.

Ron could see the toll that "deep night" was taking on Paul. Paul was physically exhausted—the calls for help from his neighbors did not stop during the days when he was trying to catch up on some sleep. Also interfering with his rest, Marina was imploring Paul daily, for her sake and the sake of the family if not for his own, to quit the police and move to California.

But despite his understanding of Paul's pain, Ron Cowart knew that he could not be an advocate for him within the police department. Ron understood, even if Paul did not, that not everyone saw his own "saintliness" in the community as a positive virtue. If Ron decided to go to bat for Paul, to break the chain of command and tell someone higher up what Paul was going through, that he was being harassed and victimized by prejudice, it would work against Paul. Those in the department who didn't like Ron, who resented the amount of attention he received from the newspaper and the television reporters, would turn any action on his part against Paul. After all, the story would go, if Paul Thai can't take a little razzing from his fellow cops, how's he going to make it on the street anyway? Does he need his daddy, Ron, to come and fight his battles for him?

Paul was not asking for that kind of help and Ron knew better than to offer it. After twenty years on the force, Cowart, eligible for early retirement, had recently been offered a job created for him by the city of Dallas. He was asked to be a liaison between the city and the police and to target the high-crime areas in Dallas and help strategize a course of action. After much agonizing over the decision, Cowart, feeling that he could ultimately be more vocal and initiate more action for the Asian community as well as the other lower income areas in the city if he were no longer a member of the Dallas Police Department, had decided to retire from the force and accept the city job. Cowart knew that as the first "coordinator of crime management" for the city of Dallas, he would be able to shape the position as he saw fit. He knew he would need a Cambodian translator as one of his assistants. Although he didn't feel that he could actively involve himself in Paul's current struggle with his FTO, Ron knew that if Paul Thai decided against finishing his training with the Dallas Police Department, he would be able to offer him a job in his new office.

When Paul visited the storefront during his "deep night" training phase, he found himself even more confused and uncertain. He was torn between wanting to return there, to once again work for Ron Cowart, whom he respected and who respected him, and to feel the working bonds that had developed among Leck Keovilay, Thao Dam, and himself. There was a new Cambodian PSO who had come in to fill the position he had vacated when he returned to the academy. Khung Ly Lim, a young Chinese–Cambodian man, a friend of Paul's, had taken his place. A brand-new United States citizen, Khung Ly was now known around the storefront as Kevin and also by his other American nickname, Bubba. Paul saw his friend Kevin working at his old job and knew that he couldn't come back and asked to be reinstated. It was more than not wanting to hurt his friend. Paul had brought honor to himself and to his family when he was accepted into the academy as a police trainee. To fail would mean to lose face privately and publicly.

Understanding Paul's dilemma is difficult for an American to thoroughly grasp. American-born Americans can easily discuss matters such as job burnout, mid-life career changes, creative differences, personality clashes, and conflicting interests as motivations to change jobs. The comfort and security of being "at home" in one's country gives one the luxury of choice. It certainly may be well argued that many American-born Americans, particularly those with the limitations imposed by a lower socioeconomic status, a poor education, and physical or mental disabilities do not enjoy the same choices as their middle-class, diploma-d and degreed, able-bodied counterparts, but for anyone who speaks the language and understands the codes embedded in the slang of popular culture, a face-saving rationale can be formulated for making a career change or more directly to the point, quitting a job.

Americans who have lived all their lives here in the United States enjoy another advantage over Paul and other new Americans. They not only understand the self-referential popular culture slang—the allusions to old and new television shows, commercials, and advertising slogans and song lyrics, as well as the fashions and the body language of their fellow Americans—but they also comprehend the cultural and geographical prejudices that exist within the United States. People who live in the northern United States can smugly point their fingers south, and no matter how hypocritical their gesture might be, accuse those living south of the Mason-Dixon Line of being racist. Pointing north, southerners can begin their own round of name-calling with carpetbagger, exploiter, and Yankee heathen ranking high on the list of insults. Prejudices exist latitudinally as well as longitudinally—the East Coast feels superior to the West Coast just as surely as blue-blooded old money looks down its patrician nose at the newest and greenest money.

Regional stereotyping is played upon for both high drama and low comedy. The plays of Tennessee Williams are as responsible for painting indelible portraits of certain types of Southern men and women as are television programs like "The Beverly Hillbillies." As soon as a character in a film, play, or television show uses a Southern accent, an Appalacian twang or a Texas drawl, audience members consciously and unconsciously call upon a series of expectations that color their appreciation and understanding of the work.

State by state or, more accurately, state versus state, this kind of stereotyping flourishes. Illinoisans refer to residents of their neighboring state, Wisconsin, as "cheese heads" because of its being the dairy state. The kind of jokes that used to be called moron jokes or, in some circles, still exist in their reincarnation as the cruel Polish jokes, are often retooled and repeated, substituting various states' residents as the jokes' victims. For example, in Ohio, someone might ask how many Kentuckians it takes to screw in a light bulb and in Texas, someone will want to know how many Okies can ride in the back seat of a Volkswagon.

This kind of stereotyping and prejudice isn't peculiarly American. In Cambodia, city dwellers felt far more westernized and sophisticated than the rural peasants and consequently far superior. And in turn, the village farmers felt their life preferable to the seminomadic tribesmen who still make their homes in the remote areas of Southeast Asia.

Since no country has a monopoly on opinion, prejudice, or stereotyping, Paul Thai is not naive about its existence. He is, however, not educated in the prejudices that are specific to the United States, nor is he necessarily aware of any of the backgrounds of these labels. He has learned about the United States Civil War, slavery and its abolition, and studied its causes and results in his college courses in American History. This gives him the beginnings of an understanding of the racial problems that continue to exist between blacks and whites.

But when asked if he feels that perhaps part of his dilemma while working for the Dallas Police Department has anything to do with the reputation of the Dallas Police Department, with any recent notoriety about racism within its ranks, Paul is completely puzzled. He has seen some behavior on the street, both on the part of cops and citizens, that seems to be sparked by racial prejudice, yet when asked if he feels Texas is any more or less hospitable to those with skin color other than white, or if he thinks that Texas is more conservative in its governmental policies toward refugees, or if, in general, the state is less "user-friendly" than any other, Paul shakes his head.

"I know a few words of American prejudice," says Paul, "let's see if I've got it right. In the states up north, the people are 'Yankees,' right? And a 'Yankee' is the same thing as a 'redneck,' right?"

The typical response of a "Yankee" might be to quickly sit up straight and righteously protest. "Of course not," yells the Pennsylvanian, "everyone knows that 'rednecks' live in the south. Or in Texas!" And that is when one begins to understand the dilemma of the social worker, the minister, the healthcare worker, and the friend of the refugee. No one wants to teach the refugees prejudice, or even teach about where the germs of prejudice first sprouted. Too often it becomes a confusing, hypocritical lesson—even for the teacher who is attempting an evenhanded, balanced account.

In the refugee camp, when Paul reported to his father that another Cambodian had told him that in Dallas, Texas, there were cowboys who would shoot you down in the street, Paul's father replied that the family would take their chances in America. It would be better than dodging the bullets and land mines of the Khmer Rouge in Cambodia. Today the cowboy story seems like a laughable and fairly harmless mythologizing of the Old West. However, in 1981, when they were waiting anxiously to leave Thailand, Paul and his father might have heard another frightening story about present-day Texas. A true story.

In the Kemah-Seabrook area of Texas, approximately thirty miles south of Houston, a group of American fishermen, angry because large numbers of Vietnamese refugees were successfully competing with them in the shrimping industry, called in the Ku Klux Klan to intimidate and threaten the Vietnamese, hoping that the sight of burning boats, figures hung in effigy, and heavily armed, robed Klansmen would scare them out of Galveston Bay. The strategy failed to work because Colonel Nam Van Nguyen, the community elder and leader, refused to be intimidated.

Through a lawsuit eventually brought on their behalf by Morris Dees of The Southern Poverty Law Center, the court ordered the American fishermen and the Klan to cease all intimidating acts. Unfortunately, the emotional scars left by a visit from the Ku Klux Klan are not easily forgotten. The lack of tolerance that brought the situation to its climax showed some ugly Americans at their ugliest. Even those area residents not directly involved with the fishing dispute allowed themselves to be quoted spouting bigotry and slinging racial epithets.

A few years later, Ron Cowart, a white Texan, Vietnam vet, would start the East Dallas Storefront to assist the Asian refugees. Both the Klan story and the Cowart story might be given equal billing on a television news magazine program. Which one shows the true heart of Texas?

If one starts to explain to Paul that many people, especially those who came of age in the late 1960s, might think the police department is a less tolerant place to work for someone of his talents and sensibilities, he will ask about his role model, Ron Cowart. Is he not a police officer? And if a smug urban liberal Northerner suggests that Texas, with its conservative political contests over who can administer a more painful death penalty, might not be the most conducive environment for career and educational advancement for someone like Paul, he can point out Texans who, in addition to Ron Cowart, have been superior friends and his conscientious supporters—Charles Kemp, Charles Morris, Melinda Cowart, John Gallagher, Larry Munoz (who tried to Americanize his honeymoon), Mack Brown (who helped start the scout troop), Ron and Shirley Decker (who took over his girl scout troop), the volunteers at the storefront, the shopkeepers who donate food for the refugee community and the Dallas-area citizen groups who volunteer time and energy.

Just as America is more idealistically seen through the eyes of its newest

immigrants and is heard to sing as inspiringly as poet Walt Whitman proclaimed it did through the ears of the refugees who gratefully hug its shores,
the American people are more clearly defined on an individual basis by their
newest friends. Although one of Paul Thai's first encounters with an American
was to watch him walk out the door with the family's new television set, his
subsequent encounters, with the people who encouraged him and became his
friends, gave him the picture of America that he believes to be the true one.
He was not naive enough to believe that all Americans were the modern-day
equivalents of the signers of the Bill of Rights. Nor was he cynical enough to
apply a salve made of sour grapes and convince himself that he could walk
away from the Dallas Police Department because they were a bunch of
bureaucrats and rednecks anyway.

"I did begin to see that there were police officers who saw things as 'black
or white,' " says Paul. "And I knew that I didn't see things that way all the
time.

"For example, at the storefront Dorsey saw some Cambodians driving a
new van and said not to give them any bags of rice when they came in. He
said they could afford a new van, so we shouldn't give them free food. On the
other hand, Ronny saw that new van differently, the way I did. We had talked
to the people and knew that a lot of families had put their money together
to buy it so they could carpool to work. When one family bought an old junky
car that they could afford by themselves, it would break down all the time and
they would miss work and lose their jobs. Then they got the idea to share the
expenses of a better car and they bought the van. It didn't mean that they were
rich. It didn't mean they didn't need our help. So Ronny would say to go
ahead and give them the rice. Dorsey would say no, don't give them the rice
because you help the neediest only until they can help themselves, then they
move on and are no longer dependent. Ronny would say that giving the rice
meant as much as a symbol of us being there to help as it did as food.

"Ronny had good points and I agreed with him. Rice means so much more
than food to Asians. It means life.

"But I also saw Dorsey's point. He made sense, too. My father often said
that Cambodians shouldn't stay on aid or take help too long or they would
get too dependent. Dorsey made sense and Ronny made sense, but they didn't
agree with each other. They were on two sides. And I was in the middle, seeing
both of the sides. But," says Paul, "I always gave the rice."

In the car with his Field Training Officer, Paul did not have the opportunity to weigh two sides of an argument. There was only one side—that of his trainer. Paul had realized in his first seven-week session of field training that each FTO creates his own world. In this third session, it was hammered home nightly that this FTO didn't think Paul would ever fit into his universe.

Looking back, Paul sees the options that were available to him during that time. "I could have gone to the Chief, but that would have been very difficult. Who would the chief believe—me or my trainer who had been on the force a long time? There was a sergeant who was in charge of all the FTOs that I could have talked to, but he got reports all the time so I thought he already knew what was going on. And the thing is, my trainer was an FTO. They had picked him to be this, so would they all say, no, we made a mistake, this is not how we want officers to train new officers? I didn't think that would happen.

"There were some other things that I thought about. For me, being a police officer was connected to going to school. I figured I could keep getting more and more college hours and get a degree. But I started thinking about being on different shifts and wondering how I could make a school schedule and stick to it.

"Also there was my work in the community. I had joined the Dallas Police Department as a PSO so I could help the people in Little Asia. At the storefront that is what I did. As a cop, I could be assigned anywhere in the Dallas area. I think I would have been assigned in East Dallas, because I think they would have needed me there for translation, but there was no guarantee of that, since they had the storefront there and they could use the PSOs. These things were all on my mind."

A defense can be made for a trainer of any kind who talks tough, handles his pupil roughly. Athletic team coaches often talk tough and abusively in order to incite their players to get mad, to play more aggressively. But this strategy does not work for every player.

A field training officer for a large urban police department can certainly make the argument that rookies have to be toughened up, hardened to the abuses they might suffer on the street. But this, too, does not work for every rookie. Paul Thai had been driven and tortured by the Khmer Rouge, some of the worst tormentors in history, and had not cracked—insults, racial slurs, and name-calling were nothing to what he had endured in his homeland. But it wasn't supposed to happen in America.

The "deep night" that Paul found himself in was even deeper and darker and more mysterious than it had first seemed. The layers of prejudice that had been buried by the idealistic notions that everything was free and equal in America were uncovered for Paul. He was learning that imagined America held a different promise that actual America. But more importantly, he was learning that even if life were not as free and equal as he had first believed, it was filled with more possibilities. In America, choices did exist.

Marina Thai was learning about choices, too. Paul returned from work one February morning to find Marina organizing their clothes and household goods, preparing to pack them. She held the children close to her, looked at Paul, the head of the household, and told him she was ready to move to California. Then she begged him to say yes, to say that they would go.

Paul knew that if he agreed, he would have to face all those friends and supporters who had celebrated his entry into the police academy. He knew that his heart would be heavy when he looked through the family photo albums and scrapbooks and saw the newspaper clippings that proclaimed him the first U.S. Cambodian police officer. He knew that he would have to choose his words carefully when he telephoned his father, so proud of his American policeman son, and explained the decision.

He looked at Marina and saw the fear in her eyes that had been there since he had been on the streets. He considered his own dream of education and freedom for himself and his children. Gathering up all the strength it would take to fight the ancient Cambodian voices telling him not to lose face, he told Marina yes, he would quit the police force, and yes, they would move to California.

10
Reinventing the Dream

There was an old man who had been a landowner in Cambodia. He operated a farm that had been in his family for centuries. When the Khmer Rouge came and took over, he refused to leave. His son had to drag him off the land. Over the next five years, his family members died or were killed—one by one they disappeared—until only the old man was left. He was the only survivor. In the refugee camp in Thailand, he was adopted by another Cambodian family. When that family got their chance to come to America, they brought the old man with them to Dallas. He did not want to come to America, did not want to leave Cambodia, but he did. Once here, he became more and more melancholy. He longed for his home. He wanted to die in Cambodia so his spirit could join the spirits of his family members. One morning he awoke to find a note from his adopted family. They had left for California and said they would send for him. But they never did. So, alone in a bare room, with only a bowl of rice on the floor, the man rocked back and forth, all day and night, praying that he could somehow return to his homeland.

A true story from Little Asia.

Paul Thai resigned from the Dallas Police Department in February, 1989. He issued no complaints about his FTO, he did not mention any discriminatory language or name-calling, he voiced no dissatisfaction with anyone in the department. He simply stated that his family feared for his safety on the street, and he had decided to move with them to California.

When Paul told Ron Cowart that he had decided to resign, Ron encouraged him to talk to someone in the department before he made a final decision. Since his first two field training officers had given him good scores, it was possible that even if he got a failing grade, as he feared he might from his third FTO, he would be able to explain the score in the light of the personality conflicts that had arisen. But for Paul, explaining his problems and discussing his decisions with any of the higher-ups in the department would have been impossible—a sign of weakness and shame. It would mean that he was not bearing responsibility for his own actions. It was a difficult enough decision for him to make the break with the Dallas Police Department. In order to do it, Paul had to make it as clean and uncomplicated as he could.

Marina was delighted. She and Paul and Chet and Maly would be reunited with the rest of their families and she could once again sleep peacefully through the night. The fears and the ghosts that had haunted her during Paul's "deep night" training would vanish. Breathing easily for the first time in months, she continued to pack and assure her mother over the telephone that they were on their way west.

While Marina organized their move, there was another movement going on—one designed to keep Paul Thai in Dallas. Sergeant Dan Bell was now in charge of the East Dallas Storefront and Ron Cowart was lobbying him to talk to Paul about staying in Texas, about returning to the storefront. Sergeant Bell agreed that Paul was a good man and that he could certainly use his services in Little Asia, so he caught up with Paul down at the central division and asked him not to quit. Paul remembers that the Sergeant was quite persistent. "When Sergeant Bell told me he needed me and asked me to come back to the storefront, I told him that I was sorry, but I was moving to California.

"Actually, I was feeling torn about everything. I didn't really want to quit the department, but because of Marina and the way 'deep night' was going, I felt like I couldn't stay. It was funny because even before my family had moved, I had been the one who wanted to go to California in the first place—when I heard that it was easier to get an education there. At least now, if we moved, I could go there and work part-time and go to school and maybe even get my degree.

"But the sergeant asked me what part of California I was moving to and I told him San Diego and he said, 'Paul, don't do it.' He said he had been born and raised there and he knew I wouldn't be able to find a job. He talked and talked about why I shouldn't go there.

"He told me I could have my old job back and no one would look down on me or anything. I could work on being more assertive while I was working at the storefront, if that's what I needed to do, but he said, please come back to work for him. I kept saying no, that I couldn't, then he made me a good offer. He told me to take three weeks vacation and go visit our families and see California and if I liked it there—and here he made a sad face—I could move there. But if I wanted to come back—then he gave a big smile—I could have my job back at the storefront. I said okay."

Paul and his family drove out to San Diego. Marina's family was delighted to see them and told them they should move there where everyone could be together again. Paul's family in Modesto was more reserved. "They told me that I should move there and be with them if that is what I wanted, but they said it might be hard for me to start over there. They knew that my life was very involved with the Little Asia community and the storefront and the police department."

Paul's father admits now that he would like for his family to all live together again. "We were separated already during the Communist time, and here in America, we should be together," he says. But Paul also understands his father believes in paying back debts. Paul's work for the police department in Dallas seemed to him to be a good way of showing America the family's gratitude.

"So I started talking more and more to Marina about this big decision we had to make," says Paul, "and finally one time when I brought it up again, she said, okay, we don't have to move to California.

"I said, what? That is all you talked about and now, so calmly, you say we don't have to move? And she said that she was just trying to get me off the street. She was upset when I worked in the night and she said that because she couldn't sleep, she felt so hopeless and afraid all the time, afraid that I would get shot out on the street.

"But now, she said, Sergeant Bell has made a good offer. He wants you back at the storefront and that won't be so dangerous. It turned out that Sergeant Bell had talked to her and offered to take her out to lunch and everything! He was smart to get Marina on his side!

"And Ron talked to me, too. He said I should come back to the storefront. And I did feel that I wanted to go back to working there. Leck and Thao, and Kevin, who had taken my place, were all pleased when I decided yes, that I would go back to the storefront. Back to PSO Thai."

As difficult as it was for Paul to go back, he was pleased with his decision to return to the storefront. He did regret, though, that he had resigned from the department during his field training. "It's just my nature, I guess, to not want to cause anyone trouble, to make things as clean and easy for everyone as I can. I should have stayed and talked over my problems with someone. I should have talked to the chief about what was going on. I should have requested a transfer.

"At the time, though, no one told me about a transfer. No one told me that such a thing was possible."

Paul found out about transferring to another division when he was caught in a familiar situation after his return to the storefront. He was called on for advice and support by Sunny Lov, a Cambodian friend who was now in police training and having a difficult time. He called Paul at the storefront and said that he couldn't take it anymore. The same isolation, loneliness, and verbal abuse that Paul had suffered were now being showered on Sunny Lov. But he had something that Paul had not had—a Cambodian role model, someone who had been through the experience before and could give him support. Sunny Lov had Paul Thai for his friend.

"Don't quit, I would say to Sunny," remembers Paul. "I told him that was my problem, that I didn't talk to anyone, that I just resigned and didn't make any waves. I told him that was my mistake and I regretted it now. I told him, now if I wanted to be an officer, I would have to try to go through the academy again. I talked and talked and talked to him.

"Finally, he said, okay, Paul, I won't quit now. I will try to stick it out for a few more weeks. Then, the next day, he would call me and say, this is it, Paul, I can't take it anymore, I am going to resign. I told him to go talk to the chief, to talk to someone about getting a transfer. That is something I didn't even know about, I didn't know that it was possible to transfer and that is something no one told me that I could do.

"But I found out about it later and when I told Sunny, he said he would try that and he did. He went and requested a transfer to another division and got it. He went through the rest of his training without another problem. Now he is a regular officer out on the street."

Paul says this with a mixture of pride and regret. He knows in his heart that as the first Cambodian to graduate from the academy, he was the pioneer and broke ground for other Cambodians such as Sunny Lov, but there are many times when he feels that he should be out there on the street with Sunny Lov, not backing him up with support from the storefront. "But," says Paul with a smile, "Marina is much happier. Whenever I mention returning to the academy again, becoming a police officer on the street again, she says that when I do that, she will move to California. Marina has a very strong feeling on this.

"But I have feelings about it, too. It is not just Marina. I feel that I am always helping my community when I am at the storefront. On the street, it is a different kind of service. It is important, but at the storefront, I do things for Cambodians who need help, and they can only be helped by another Cambodian. This is changing because so many are moving away from the neighborhood. But still, it is the neediest who remain in Little Asia."

The East Dallas Asian neighborhood that, at its peak in 1980 and 1981, was home to four thousand Southeast Asians, has changed dramatically in the past ten years. Although it is still referred to as Little Asia by many of the health care workers, social workers, and agency and church volunteers who have been visiting there for several years, the population is no longer primarily Asian. Approximately 1,500 Southeast Asian residents remain. Asian restaurants, groceries, and a few gift stores provide a small living for their owners, but there is no tourist trade, no hustle and bustle of a big-city Chinatown.

One Southeast Asian restaurant, Mekong, was given a rave review in a 1989 *Chicago Tribune* article on places to go and things to see when visiting Dallas. Most evenings, however, this excellent, reasonably priced restaurant is almost empty. "At lunchtime they do a good business," says Paul, "but at night, Dallas people don't want to come into this neighborhood. They are afraid of Little Asia. They hear about the crime and they think it's a scary place, a dirty place. Maybe they don't trust Asian food?" Paul is surprised to hear that in other urban areas such as New York and Chicago, Asian food is not only popular, but that spicy Thai cuisine (similar to Cambodian cooking) is sought after and considered fashionable.

Paul understands why some Dallas citizens might be afraid to come into the Peak-Bryant area. It was always a poor place, a neighborhood where too many people had to share too many small spaces. It was an area where its residents were at the mercy of landlords who allowed their renters to roast in the Dallas summer heat and freeze in the damp cold of winter.

But now it's an area where gangs fight for turf. Drug dealers are seen openly doing their business, then disappearing into an uninviting courtyard. Suspicious-looking cars with opaque glass windows cruise slowly down the streets. Cambodians who may have awakened in the night to hear the ghosts of their ancestors visit their apartments now wake in the night to hear gunshots in the street.

The East Dallas Community Police and Refugee Affairs Office also reflects the changes of the neighborhood it serves. Paul, Leck, Thao, and Kevin have been joined by another PSO. Ernestine Gaitan, who left another city agency to come to the storefront, now sits at a front desk that is almost constantly surrounded with Spanish-speaking families who live in the area and require assistance from the storefront. Ernestine is in the same constant motion as the Asian PSOs—translating forms and letters, talking to landlords, employers, and welfare agencies—this time in Spanish.

Ron Cowart retired from the Dallas Police Department in spring of 1989 to become the crime manager for the city of Dallas. As Paul Thai returned to the storefront, his mentor, Ron Cowart, departed. When Ron packed up his desk, he took down the eight-by-ten-inch black-and-white photographs he had taken of area residents and carefully wrapped up the dozens of paintings done by a young Cambodian, Sareth Seng, that were graphic depictions of the bloody childhood memories he had of the killing fields. Ron's corner space seemed curiously empty, oddly black and white.

Ron had been a Dallas cop for twenty years and knew that when he left, things would change. The storefront had been part of his vision of community police work. It was not a vision shared by the entire department. With Ron officially gone, storefront policy and practice would change even more rapidly and more drastically than they had over the years.

When the storefront first opened, it was just Ron and Paul, Leck and Thao. They handled the police work and anything and everything else that needed doing in the community. They were the police, but they were also the friends, the advocates for the Little Asia residents.

Now, with a sergeant and two corporals staffing the storefront, officers who were not in favor of handing out bags of rice over the front counter, officers who maintained that there was no room for social work in a police station, Cowart knew that the storefront would become less and less the operation that he had begun in 1985.

Knowing that Paul was often teased about his loyalty to him, Ron worried about what would happen after he left. The other officers referred to Ron as Paul's "daddy" and although Paul's face remained impassive and he took the teasing like a good sport, he found himself in an uncomfortable situation. "I did feel that in some ways Ron was like a father," says Paul, "but not just to me, but to all the people in the community. He was a hero to us. He was like a saint to us.

"But it wasn't that we felt that way for no reason. When no one was helping the Asians, when no one could even speak English or even know how to ask for help, Ron came and he helped us. He did not say, 'go learn English and ask me in my language,' or 'go learn to be an American, then come to me.' He met people in the middle—people who were just beginning in America. He did save many people who felt lost and lonely, who were hungry and scared, and who couldn't find a way to help themselves."

Ron offered Paul a job in his new office. It would mean a raise in pay, and a leap forward in prestige. And to the surprise of those who teased Paul so unmercifully about being Ron's follower, his "son," his shadow, Paul turned it down.

"I had resigned from the police department and I didn't always feel good about that. I would think, maybe I shouldn't have quit, I should have talked to someone, found out about a transfer. But because I could come back to the storefront, it felt like the decision worked out okay. At the storefront, I could really help my people, really serve the community. That felt like what I should be doing. If I worked for Ronny, it would be good, too, but I would have to not only concentrate on Little Asia, I would have to work on projects that weren't involved there. It just didn't feel like the right thing to do at that time.

"And if I worked at the storefront, I could go to school. I was taking courses and getting closer to getting my associate's degree. This was a dream I couldn't give up."

Paul continued his courses at El Centro Junior College in downtown Dallas. He laughs when he talks about one of his electives. "I am still learning English, always learning more English, but I decided to take another language. Spanish! I decided I had better try to learn some while I'm working at the storefront—I can use it there because of the growing Hispanic community."

Although Little Asia is becoming less and less Asian, the Dallas business community has now decided to step into the area and capitalize on its ethnicity. Plans have been drawn up to build the Peak-Bryant Market in the heart of the square-mile neighborhood. In the earliest stages of development, the plans were directed toward making a kind of tourist attraction out of Little Asia, building stores and restaurants and drawing both Dallas residents and tourists into the area which would be developed as one comparable to San Francisco's Chinatown. The problem that necessarily arose was that ten years earlier, the area truly was a "Little Asia." Today, Asians are moving into other areas of Dallas, to suburbs such as Garland, and heading out of state, to California, where so many Cambodians have settled and written back glowing reports of their lives there. Asians are rapidly becoming a minority in the neighborhood. The planners of the new development revised their Asian marketplace, renamed it the Peak-Bryant Market and anticipate that it will encompass all the ethnic groups that make up the community. Although there are a few Asian business people in the community who feel that it will boost their business, there are others whose feelings are mixed.

"You see, some of the people in the community are afraid of such a development, they are afraid that if the area is modernized that all the rents will go up," explains Paul, "and if the rents go up, they will have to move. There are many families who still share apartments, live together the way our family did, and if they have to move to another part of the city, it probably will not be allowed. They even fear that here in the Little Asia neighborhood, if things get so improved—the way they appear on the drawings of the new development—that the landlords will say this place is so nice now, only one family can live here. Even now it is difficult to improve living conditions. A friend of mine has five children and he wanted to move to a better apartment building and when he talked to the landlord about renting a two-bedroom apartment, which was all he thought he needed and all he could afford, the landlord said, no, you must rent a four-bedroom. My friend came back very sad and said he could never afford to move anywhere.

"It looks to me like the people who are involved with developing the market are mostly Anglo. There are a few Asians, a few Hispanics who seemed to have something to do with it. There was a meeting in the community and the Anglo businessmen spoke and assured everyone that it would be good for the neighborhood. They showed the drawings of what this beautiful development would look like. They promised that everything would be okay.

"But I have seen nothing in writing. We've just heard them speak at the meeting. It's hard for me to believe that they will build this beautiful marketplace and allow everything around it to stay the same. It's hard to believe that with all the improvements, there won't be higher rents to go with them."

There is still only a small percentage of Asians in Dallas who have become United States citizens. Because there is no Asian voting block, no real Asian constituency, the Asians have no political power or real protection for their interests through the vote. Paul says that from time to time, candidates will visit the area and speak to the Cambodian Lions' Club or the Cambodian

Association, but since only around ten percent of the Cambodians have been naturalized, there is limited interest in their support.

Paul encourages his countrymen and women to get involved in the community, and to become American citizens, but there is resistance. There are those who still believe that it will be possible to return to Cambodia. And there are those who believe that they should be grateful to the United States for accepting them in the first place and that they should ask for no more—not even citizenship or the rights and privileges that come with it.

"I always remind people, when they talk about returning to Cambodia, of the life they had there," says Paul. "I tell them that even if they have a hard life here in America, there are still some things that are so much better here. One thing that they understand is when I mention 'ice' to them. I remind them that in Cambodia, they had to buy ice. In America, ice is free—you can make it in your own refrigerator."

Paul believes in grass roots movements and strongly urges people to stick together to improve conditions. He believes that a community can make any situation better. But he knows that the Little Asia area has become an almost impossible situation for most residents. "My children, Chet and Maly, told me that they saw a man who lives in the building next door go into his apartment. They said he carries a big gun in his pocket. They have seen it themselves. I know they are telling the truth because this man is a known drug dealer. And he probably knows I work in the storefront. So I know that we will have to move. It's just not safe for us to stay there.

"I know it probably sounds contradictory, but I have always been happy for people when they can move out of the neighborhood. I do want them to try to make the community better when they are there, to improve their lives and their neighbors' lives, but when they can get out and move on to find a better life, that is good, too. When they assimilate, it's better—their children can learn English faster. The parents can learn more about American culture and customs. I want my people to learn American ways. People can benefit more by doing that rather than just staying together crowded and afraid."

Paul does not confuse assimilation with the old melting pot metaphor. "This neighborhood is much more like a tossed salad. All the ingredients are put in the same bowl, but the carrots stay carrots and the radishes stay radishes," says Paul.

Nor does he fall into the confused romanticism of the Anglo who, on a Saturday afternoon, might wander through an urban Asian neighborhood, looking for exotic food, imagining the mysterious wisdom of the East—imagining that these new immigrants are happily together, keeping their culture intact.

"Sometimes, when people stay together all the time, they stay living in the past, the sad, sad past," says Paul. "They can't get beyond that. They stay together and talk about the communist time and they stay isolated. I don't believe in staying together like that.

"I understand about keeping culture alive—nobody is going to get my culture away from me. I will remember my language, my customs, my traditions. But I don't believe in having a Cambodian town where we just keep to our Cambodian ways and forget about being Americans. No. I want everyone to assimilate, to learn new ways, to be Cambodian–Americans. I like that—Cambodian–Americans. I think that is the way one must live here. You can't live in your own world and just say, 'I'm a Cambodian, not an American.' Things won't work that way."

Paul received his Associate Degree in Criminal Justice from El Centro College on May 10, 1990. Although his parents were not able to come from California to see him graduate, his friends took pictures so he could send them to his family.

Even though Paul is still the only United States citizen in his family, his brothers and his sister are doing well. Mao Thai, Paul's oldest brother, is in college in California. After classes he has a part-time job working in his brother Tang Thai's video store in Modesto. Chandy, Paul's only sister, also helps out in her brother's store after her college classes. Chandy plans on becoming an accountant.

Bun, Chi, and Pheap Thai are all living and working in the Dallas area with their wives and children. Number nine son, Many, is fourteen, in middle school in Modesto with his parents. "My parents worry about him all the time. He is at a difficult age," says Paul. "There are many distractions from school."

"My number two brother, Muy Thai, is still in Cambodia. Although we received a videotape from him and he said in it that he was okay, he didn't look very good. He looked very thin, very old. It is hard to tell what is really happening, because we know that people there aren't really free to talk about conditions there," says Paul. "My father sent him some money, but we don't always know what happens when we send anything."

Paul, as a United States citizen, would someday like to sponsor his brother and his family to come to the United States. The family assumes, however, that Muy is not in a position where he can freely express interest in coming to America. It can also be assumed that many Cambodians who are still in their country feel they are in a desperate situation.

"When we first came to America, we had someone take our picture all together, then we mailed it to the American Red Cross and some other organizations and asked that it be posted so our brother Muy might be able to find us and contact us," says Paul. "After quite a while, we got a letter from someone who said he was our brother. He said in the letter that he needed money so my father sent him some. After a while, because of some of the things he said in the letter, we got suspicious. We asked him questions, to see if he really was our brother, and he wrote back a sad letter admitting that he was just pretending.

"It made us so sad for two reasons. One reason was that we had not found our brother, Muy, and the other reason was that this man had been so desperate to have to do this. My father sent him a little money even though he wasn't our brother, but told him not to write again."

For those who might be surprised that Paul's father expressed sympathy rather than outrage, Paul is quick to point out that they have not forgotten how bad life was in Cambodia and in the camps. Since the family could spare a little money to help someone, they sent it. That person, stuck in an impossible situation in Cambodia, could have been any one of them. It could have been Muy Thai. And under different conditions, in different times, this desperate liar could have been a friend.

"In Cambodia, after the restaurant was closed, my mother used to tell us children stories at bedtime," says Paul. "Even when we came here—sometimes when it was so hot in that first summer in Dallas, she would go from one of us to the other at bedtime, sponging us off and telling us Cambodian folktales. One of my favorite stories was about the ants and the worm. It was a story that was in many Cambodian schoolbooks.

"The worm was a very poor and ugly creature and had no friends except the ants. The ants would be nice to him and help him find food. But the other animals looked down on the worm, thought it was a nasty animal. They would say, 'Look at you, worm, you have no backbone.' But the ants never called him names and were good friends to him. One day, the worm turned into a butterfly and everybody made a big fuss over him, about how beautiful he was, and the butterfly was so happy about that he didn't pay any attention to the ants anymore. He didn't like the ants, the same ones who used to help him.

"It was a sad thing for the ants, when the worm went off and forgot about them. My mother would always say that it meant that if we ever became rich, we should never forget our friends—the old friends who helped us before."

Epilogue

And That Is Freedom

Political Democracy, as it exists and practically works in America, with all its threatening evils, supplies a training school for making first class men. It is life's gymnasium, not of good only, but of all.
                    —Walt Whitman, *Democratic Vistas,* 1871

You have reached WAR, White Aryan Resistance.
Well, White Man, San Diego is really getting yellow. Natural City looks like Cambodia. Do you realize that the Asians are the most dangerous threat to the existence of our race? The United States is being overrun by these Gook-eyed Asians: Phillipinos, Vietnamese, Chinese, Japs, Koreans, bringing their culture to the shores of America. Oh, yes, they will smile at you and act real friendly. So will a rattlesnake. Given half a chance they will cut your throat in a minute. This yellow mass from the East, the Gookizing of America, intermixing with a white, the planned destruction of the Aryan race. The white youth of this country being shipped overseas and bringing back these skinny, ugly Asian wives and producing nonwhite offspring. While this horde of Asiatic parasites invade this nation, setting up their own communities like Little Saigon in Orange County and Little Tokyo in LA. Did you know that in Long Beach they have the biggest Cambodian community outside of Cambodia itself? These Gooks are getting government loans to set up their communities and businesses and invading this country like a bunch of rats while our own white people are starving in the streets of the country they fought and died for. White children going hungry because their parents don't have the money to feed them. The Zionist Occupational Government doesn't give a damn about those Vietnam Veterans who lost their limbs and lives and were poisoned by Agent Orange in Vietnam and are dropping like flies. What a national disgrace. Why if we had people like our forefathers, we would organize in the streets and run these dog-eaters from the shores of this nation. We need to cleanse this nation of all nonwhite mud-races for the very survival of our own people and the future generations of our children. Now it's time. Join with us, WAR, White Aryan Resistance and let the battle begin.
                    —right-wing recorded message, May 23, 1988

185

Assignment: A descriptive essay about a familiar place

The Storefront
by Pov Thai
English 101, El Centro College, 6/17/87

They call it the storefront, but it's really more than that. The building itself is old and falling apart. The paint is flaking off the wall, the ceiling is high and lofty, but sometimes it would be better if there were no ceiling at all, because the rain leaks in but it can't leak out.

The carpet is grey, dingy, and ratty. It stinks from old rainfall and leftover food, and everything looks dirty in the bluish fluorescent lights. Your voice is amplified by the hard walls and high ceiling.

On walking into the building, you do not feel invited in. There is a big barrier that you have to walk around to get inside the office. While you are walking around this obstacle you notice all the desks are staring at you, then you squeeze past the couch and you discover yourself in a long aisle that leads past the staring desks which wink at you metalically.

If you look to the left side you will see big Vietnamese and Cambodian flags hung on the wall along with the American and Texas flags which are stuck up on a stick on either side of Sergeant Parker's desk.

For some unknown reason there is a large plate heaped full of rice which is spilling over onto his desk. There seems to be an invasion of rice in this place. In the back, there are five tons of rice, mostly bagged. Recently there was as much as twenty tons of rice but most of it has trickled out the door. Sometimes when the rice escapes from its bag and you are walking in the back, it sounds like you are Indiana Jones walking on insects.

The only thing that is more of a mess than the rice is the mass of clothing in the opposing corner. These two things seem to have a daily contest to see who can control more of the floor. It is almost like a battle between two armies trying to take up more territory. Posters are hung all over saying PLEASE KEEP THIS PLACE CLEAN. But they are old signs and no one pays any attention to them any more.

The people that braved it past the counter, the couch, the staring desks, come in waves, like the tides of the sea. Just like a wave, they come in, pause, swirl around, stirring up debris, and then they retreat.

These people who came and left like the tide are mostly women and children. They are shorter and have darker skin than most Americans, they have jet black hair and most don't speak English. The come in with confused, lost or worried expressions and leave with a smile, and sometimes, a bag of the ever-spreading rice.

If you ever step in this place, you will think it looks like you are in China. There are strange smells and strange noises. These people are refugees.

The men who are sitting behind the staring desks are policemen. They look bigger than they really are because they wear bulletproof vests. Because of their uniforms, they look mean and tough. But they aren't. Officer Cowart looks like the Chief of Police because he is always bickering about getting programs started, keeping the place clean, and about his officers being late to work. But if you look closely, you will find him smiling and playing with the kids, or maybe practicing his Cambodian.

It is an unusual police station, but it is the storefront, and I work here.

When Walt Whitman praised democratic America as "life's gymnasium" he was not merely a starry-eyed stirrer of the melting pot. He had lived through the Civil War, nursed the wounded on its battlefields. He knew the evils of slavery, the attitudes of slaveholders, and must have encountered those who believed in the natural superiority of the white race. But still he found that the strengths and joys and raw beauty of America prevailed. It is hard to imagine, though, any poet who celebrated America and its infinite diversity not having the poetry knocked out of him if he were to run up against one of the venomous hate groups that have sprung up in today's United States—a group such as White Aryan Resistance.

Benjamin Franklin, Washington Irving, Ralph Waldo Emerson, Henry David Thoreau . . . all the writers who make up the Early American literary history—the very writers whom Paul Thai is assigned to read in his college English classes—describe an America of inestimable beauty, range, and possibility. Paul's father's belief that America meant freedom and education can easily be found in the writings of these early poets and philosophers. Both Emerson and Thoreau, American Transcendentalists, believed in and espoused Eastern teachings. Thoreau's *Walden* is a handbook on living in harmony with nature—a belief that is as natural to Cambodians as breathing.

The Southeast Asian refugees who formed their ideas of America and Americans by watching the tireless volunteers in the border camps, by listening to Christian pastors who paid them individual attention, and who learned their English and their daily living skills for survival in America from the selfless caseworkers and neighborhood volunteers, indeed have a rose-tinted vision of Americans. They have seen some of the best and the bravest. Yet, as long as we American-born Americans continue to define ourselves through baseball, mom, and apple pie; as long as we continue to teach our children the poetry that proclaims democracy a "training school for first-class men"; and as long as we allow the Statue of Liberty to display her message of welcome to the immigrants and the refugees all over the world, we, too, will continue to deny that the rosy vision is in any way faded or discolored.

It is not Asian politeness that makes Paul Thai uncritical of America. It is his meticulous study and observation. Even though Americans are masters of parody and self-deprecation, even though American protests and letters to the editor and cynicism about elected officials are legendary, it is still obvious to Paul and any other new American that the underlying strength of the United States is in its imagined glory. No matter how high the taxes, the crime rate, or the utilities bill—no matter the number of homeless and helpless—Americans still manage to carry on a romance with America. Movies, music, television, sports, and retail stores all sell an image of America that is consumed daily. If one can only wear the right shirt with the right logo, if one can drink the right brand of beer, smoke the right cigarette, drive the right car, one can be an American. One can have that happiness reflected on the billboards and in the commercials. If Americans believe that, if they buy that, how can the newest Americans not believe it, too?

Today, the refugees no longer come through the door at the East Dallas Storefront in waves. The dwindling Asian population accounts, in part, for that. Many of the refugees miss Ron Cowart welcoming them in from his big corner desk. Lynn Dorsey and Sergeant Bell were also familiar faces who have now been transferred to other divisions. Paul, Leck, and Thao are still there along with the newer PSOs, Ernestine and Kevin. Periodically, volunteers from churches and community service groups arrive, bringing a casserole lunch for the staff and smiles and good cheer for the refugees whom they've come to meet and invite to their church services.

For several months during 1990, the rice that was such an important symbol of friendship and nourishment, the rice that meant life to the Asians, was no longer bagged and given out at the storefront. People who came in and said they were hungry and needed food were directed to the appropriate social service agencies and churches. The limited amount of food supplies that were stocked on a shelf in the back of the storefront were kept only for emergencies.

Paul isn't clear exactly why the rice reappeared at the storefront. There were many protests when the rice was not given out, but no one knows for sure whose complaint was finally heard. Most people in the neighborhood believe, as usual, that their friend, Ron Cowart, had something to do with it. The storefront now operates strictly by the book say those who work there. Refugees fill out forms at the front counter or at a PSO's desk when they come in for assistance. If the storefront staff can help, they do. If they can direct the refugees to the right agency where they can get what they need, they will. No one lounges on the couch by the front window. No longer the hub of a lively, if confused, community, the storefront has a more efficient look, a less chaotic ambience.

Leck, Kevin, and Paul are all taking college classes in addition to working at the storefront. They all laugh when anyone mentions the "miracle minority" or the fact that Asians are so smart, such good students, that it must be easier for them to balance education, job, and family than it is for others.

Kevin Lim, who escaped from Cambodia with his father and his sister—his mother, a teacher, was killed by the Khmer Rouge—describes taking a college test. "My wife is Chinese and she is a Christian. I am Cambodian–Chinese and I was raised in Buddhism, so my method for taking an exam is to pray to Jesus and to pray to Buddha"—Kevin pauses and leans forward seriously—"then to study real, real hard."

Paul laughs and agrees. "One time, a Mexican guy who was walking out of class with me was talking to me and asked me why Asians were so smart, why I didn't have to study. I just looked at him and asked him if he was kidding or what? I told him I studied until two or three in the morning sometimes just to get a passing grade.

"I told him that being an Asian didn't make me smarter. But I also told him this—that sometimes Asian refugees will work very hard because, to us, school and studies mean life. He asked me what I meant and I told him we came here without language or education. Couldn't get any decent jobs. And if we can't work, we can't eat. If we can't eat, we will die. We are studying for our lives."

Paul and Kevin also emphasize the family pressure to study. Asians believed that they had to do well in school to bring honor to their families. "Also, people should remember that our teachers beat us up when we didn't do well. And our parents did, too, sometimes. That helped to motivate studying, too," adds Paul.

In order to dispel the "model minority" myth, the National Conference of Christians and Jews, the Asian American Journalists Association and the Association of Asian Pacific American Artists have produced an eighty-page booklet for those in the media, "Asian Pacific Americans: A Handbook on How to Cover and Portray Our Nation's Fastest Growing Minority Group."

The manual explains that although many of the old media stereotypes—the Yellow Peril, Charlie Chan or geisha girls—have disappeared from use, they have been replaced with new stereotypes such as the "model minority" of academically and economically successful Asians. These stereotypes do not allow for many of the facts surrounding the different Asian groups.

The Koreans, for example, who are touted as being such successful green-grocers and shopkeepers in some of the poorer, predominantly black urban neighborhoods, are often discovered to be professionals with advanced degrees from their own countries, locked out of their fields in the United States, victims of prejudice themselves. Their incomes are relatively higher than other community members because they work longer hours and use all family members as workers in their businesses. Just as the Vietnamese fishermen in the Seabrook, Texas, area were accused of "overfishing" Galveston Bay, Koreans and other Asians are accused of being "overachievers" who are robbing American-born Americans of jobs and dollars.

It is a rude awakening indeed for Asians who, studying American literature, see similarities between their own cultural and religious beliefs and the Protestant work ethic that is so prevalent in early American writings and become enamored with the idea that any American can grow up to be president, that a penny saved is a penny earned, and that a stich in time saves nine. The American literary canon paints a portrait of Americans such as Benjamin Franklin's Poor Richard, who teaches that whoever is clever, curious, thrifty, inventive and hardworking will be rewarded. Asian students in their early English classes might read Ralph Waldo Emerson and Henry David Thoreau and feel attuned to the American appreciation of nature, only to find out that Americans have destroyed much of the natural landscape and created a new one by piling up nonbiodegradable garbage into dumps and landfills.

Many Asians who are new Americans, studying and working hard to be successful in their new countries, still believe in an "imagined America" one created and described by literature, music, art, and their own dreams and myths of this country of freedom and education. The belief remains strong in spite of the refugees' poverty, isolation, and the frequent prejudiced rage directed toward them.

Paul, more street smart than many of his countrymen and women, is still confused by the idealism and consumerism that make up American culture. "The first time I saw a shelf in a drugstore filled with all those bottles of shampoo and conditioner and hair rinses, I was amazed. It wasn't just that there were so many, although that was amazing, too, but it was that the containers were so beautiful. I figured that you bought the container, then after you used all of the shampoo, you brought it back and refilled it.

"I could not believe that you were supposed to just throw such a beautifully made bottle away. In Cambodia, you were so happy if you got a coconut because if you found one, you got to eat the meat of it and drink the milk, but even more important, you got to keep the shell and could make a cup. You owned something permanent.

"But in America, it's good, I guess, that you use these things and throw them away because it must be cheap to make more? And this gives people jobs, right? So it must be good?"

Paul is interested when he hears about recycling efforts, about renewed concern for depleted resources, and is aware of the media attention that surrounds conservation and environmental issues, but explains that some worries shared by Americans are not yet worries that can be fully understood by new Americans.

"For some of us, it is like a discussion of calories and cholesterol," explains Paul patiently. "I see Americans read the labels on boxes to find out about calories and fat and salt and sugar and everything that goes into foods. This is good. They know how to take care of themselves and they are protecting their health.

"But with Marina and me," Paul says, "if it tastes good, we eat it. We don't care about calories and cholesterol. We believe in moderation in food and drinking because that is just our way, but we don't care about the rest of that stuff. We starved for years. For years, our one meal of the day was a bowl of watery rice, so when people start asking about how many calories are in something or if something we are eating is fattening, we don't know. We don't care.

"I see commercials about fitness, about health clubs and exercise. This is good because you should take care of your body and exercise some, but I know some guys in the police department, guys I knew at the academy who went to a real popular health club, the President's Club every day, all the time when they weren't at work. That is all they talked about. It was hard for me to understand why someone would want to do that all the time, why they wouldn't want to take some classes for education or read a book or be with their families."

When an American asked Amos Oz, the Israeli writer, why he still smoked cigarettes, knowing they were so bad for his health, he said, "Give us a few years of peace in our country, then we will have the time and the energy to worry about quitting smoking."

Paul feels that American-style health-consciousness, whether exhibited as calorie counting or pumping iron, is at least a generation away for Cambodians. "Even regular health care is a kind of luxury for us. A lot of the nurses, the health care workers who come and make home visits in the community, ask me what is the matter with your people? They say we don't want to take care of our health or take medicine seriously, but it is really because of the differences in our cultures. In Cambodia there were not a lot of hospitals and the ones that were there were in the cities. Most of the people who are here now are from villages and the farming countryside, so some people have never even seen a hospital.

"The nurses will give some medicine or tell a mother she should bring her child back for immunization on a certain day, and the mother doesn't do it. She doesn't keep up the medicine or the shots and the nurse thinks she doesn't care.

"I have to explain to her that other things come up, other worries, that prevent the mother from coming back. In our culture, we don't put health care as the number-one thing the way Americans do. In America, someone gets sick and says, right away, that he has to go to the doctor.

"I have always had migraine headaches and sometimes when I was young I would have a headache, not be able to open my eyes, and my parents would give me folk medicines and then they would not worry too much or take it real seriously. Maybe I shouldn't say this, but some Americans seem to have a heart attack when they get the flu.

"In our country there were so many other things to worry about. Like, will we have food tomorrow? Is the Khmer Rouge in the next town and will they be in our town tomorrow? Are Americans going to drop bombs tomorrow?

Then maybe we get the flu. Are we going to worry about the flu or are we going to worry about more important things, like, will we be alive tomorrow?"

After living there nearly ten years, Paul Thai moved out of the Little Asia area of Dallas. The family's new apartment on Stretch Drive is close to some other Cambodian families, but it does not hold the same familiar warmth that the Peak-Bryant area represented for him in his first years in America. "There was actually a shootout between drug dealers in the apartment building next door to us," says Paul. "It just got too scary for my family to be in Little Asia. Too many criminals."

The neighborhood may turn around if the plans are carried out for the new Peak-Bryant Marketplace. Creating an open-air ethnic shopping mall, drawing in tourists and visitors from the entire Dallas area might force a cleanup of the entire place, razing some of the tenement buildings, and forcing out the addicts and dealers who operate out of them. If it also forces out some Asian families—a few Asian businesses too small to afford rental space in the new market—it will be figured into the price extracted for progress. It's not hard to imagine the "Yuppification" of the East Dallas area which will probably then be accurately referred to as the *former* Little Asia neighborhood.

Paul worries about the families still in Little Asia. He will continue to serve the community by working at the storefront as long as he can. Even when he wasn't officially working at the storefront, during his months at the academy, people in need called on him for help. They found him wherever he was. They will still find him since he plans on spending as much time volunteering in the community as he always did.

Paul and Marina have been able to take vacations out West, to visit their families in California. Although he says that they are Texans, Paul admits that he loves the ocean and they would like someday to live near the sea. Paul and Marina have taken Chet and Maly to Disneyland and Sea World and they've played slot machines in Reno. They bought a used van for family trips.

At home the children watch tapes of traditional Cambodian dance, Chinese movies dubbed in Cambodian and *The Little Mermaid* on their VCR, and Chet and Paul compete at Nintendo. Paul recently bought a 35-mm camera and a used computer, an IBM compatible, that he can use for his homework. Marina watches her soap operas and likes to listen to George Michael and Madonna on the stereo. The family's telephone answering machine offers a simple message—twice—first in Paul's flawless English, then in perfect Khmer.

Paul would like, someday, to buy a house with a yard for a garden and a play area for the children. "It would not have to be a big house like some Americans have," says Paul. "I did not believe it when I went to a party at a police officer's house and saw all the rooms that he and his wife had that they didn't use. It was a five-bedroom house for two people. He took me around and showed me all the rooms, flicked the light switch on and there's a room all decorated and furnished and he said they never used that room. I couldn't believe it."

With the help of his friends Barbara Boyd and Charles Kemp, Paul completed his application to the University of Texas at Dallas, was accepted, and is now taking a full course load there. He admits that he would like to get his bachelor's degree, but characteristically shakes his head and says, "I don't know if I can, but I will try."

Paul still dreams of being a teacher. He does act as an instructor when as a PSO he is asked to speak at various schools about his own experiences as a refugee. He is articulate and persuasive as he speaks to students about the privileges and responsibilities of being an American. He says that these speaking engagements, these teaching sessions are his favorite duty.

Paul encourages his son, Chet, and his daughter, Maly, to speak English at every opportunity. When asked if he wants them to act in a typically American manner when he and Marina are older and need assistance from their children, Paul shakes his head. "I do not like to criticize America, but one thing we never had in Cambodia was nursing homes for old people. I would like Chet and Maly to have good American lives and to be good Cambodian–American children when Marina and I are old.

"There are many American ways that I observe that I like better than the Cambodian ways, though. When I see American women interact and speak their opinions on things, I think that is good. It is something I have to learn, to be better about letting Marina speak up.

"I also love the way Americans treat their children. They are patient and they ask their opinions about things. That is good. When American children answer a question, they say 'because.' They are encouraged to reason things out, not just to obey. That is good, too. They talk about their feelings. And American parents show affection to their children and tell them that they love them. I want to learn not to just be a strict father, as my father was, but also to let my children know how much I love them.

"I still want them to be respectful to me. It might be that we have to blend some Cambodian discipline with the American way of affection. We can't be all American right away. That would be impossible.

"The best thing to do is to take some good things from the American culture and some good things from the Cambodian culture. We have to be Cambodian–American—that is the way for us."

At the home of American friends, Paul watched a two-hour television special celebrating the anniversary of the satirical comedy show "Saturday Night Live," a program he had never seen. Some of the clips, particularly those with broad slapstick humor, seemed funny to him. Other sketches that relied on references to American popular culture with which he was unfamiliar were meaningless to him.

One short blackout sketch involved a cast member playing a reporter who mistook George Bush's wife, Barbara, for the president's mother. It was a short, obvious joke that referred to her appearance, gray haired and matronly, something that was constantly pointed out and picked apart by the media during the presidential campaign.

Paul reacted to this sketch with shock. To make sure he understood the joke, he asked, "That is not a compliment in this country, right? Americans don't respect age the way Cambodians do, right?" After Paul was assured that, as he thought, Americans worship youth, not age, and that it was a joke, a rude one, at the First Lady's expense, he shook his head in wonderment. "In Cambodia, if you insulted a president's wife or, for example, Sihanouk's wife, you would be killed."

Paul paused for a moment and furrowed his brow. "I guess this is America," he said softly, "and that is freedom."

Reality 1991

In mid-November 1990, Paul Thai sat and talked with his friend Sunny Lov. As he always did, Sunny encouraged Paul to come back to the regular force, to be a police officer. If Paul did want to try again to be a rookie cop, he would have to go back to the academy and once again go through field training. Sunny and Paul laughed about Paul going through the academy for a third time.

Paul told Sunny how much he enjoyed his studies at the University of Texas at Dallas. Even though his classes in Western traditions, Greek tragedy, and literary analysis were difficult, Paul was working hard and doing well. Tuition was expensive. The cost of the books was high. But Paul was getting his beloved education.

Sunny begged Paul to reconsider the police department. "We Asians have to have more representation on the force," Sunny told Paul, "and you and I, we could work together." Paul told Sunny that he agreed, that it was important for the young Cambodian kids, the ones who were dropping out of school left and right, to have a role model in the community—one that they could recognize as one of them. Paul promised his friend that he would think seriously about it.

The next day, Sunny Lov was on duty at an automobile accident site. He was setting up barricades when an oncoming car sped up, crashing into Sunny Lov, killing him instantly. Officers discovered that the driver who hit Sunny was in a stolen car and panicked when he saw a uniformed officer slowing down traffic.

Paul spent the next week comforting Sunny's widow and three young children. It was the week of Thanksgiving for most of the nation and a week of mourning for the Cambodian community of Dallas.

Just before Christmas, Paul received his semester grades: two Bs and an A. He also signed up to take the entrance exam for the police academy. In January 1991, Paul carefully talked over the situation with Marina, and she agreed with him. There should be a Cambodian on the Dallas police force. Paul had promised Sunny that he would consider coming back.

He would keep his promise.

On February 11, 1991, Paul Thai entered the Dallas Police Academy for the third time.

For Further Reading:

A Cambodian Odyssey by Haing Ngor, Macmillan, 1987.

Strangers From a Different Shore by Ronald Takaki, Little, Brown, 1989.

The Spirit of Survival by Gail Sheehy, William Morrow, 1986.

The Death and Life of Dith Pran by Sidney Schanberg, Penguin, 1985.

Cambodian Witness by Someth May, Random House, 1986

The Stones Cry Out by M. Syzmusiak, Hill and Wang, 1986

About the Author

Sharon Sloan Fiffer received a BFA at the University of Illinois at Urbana and her Master's Degree in English at the University of Illinois at Chicago. She teaches literature, creative writing, and studies in American popular culture at Barat College in Lake Forest, Illinois.

Ms. Fiffer has been the recipient of literary awards for her short fiction and received an artist's fellowship for advancement in fiction from the Illinois Arts Council in 1986. Her nonfiction has appeared in *Chicago* magazine, the *Chicago Tribune,* and *Inside Sports.* She is the coeditor of *Other Voices,* an international award-winning literary magazine. In her capacity as both a writer and editor, she has moderated and appeared on several panels discussing both fiction and nonfiction writing, editing, and publishing.

Ms. Fiffer lives in Evanston, Illinois, with her husband, writer Steve Fiffer, and their three children, Kate, Nora and Robert.